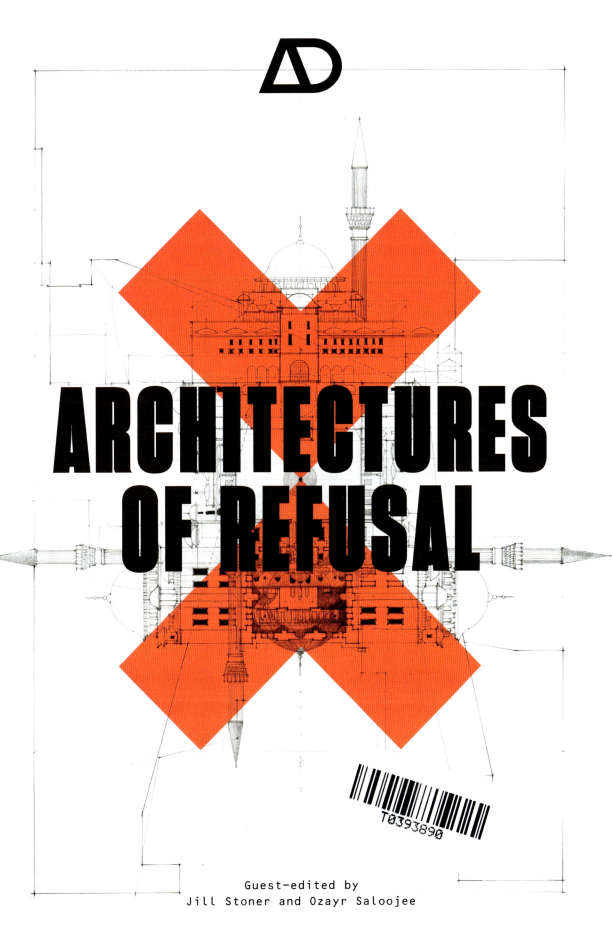

ARCHITECTURES OF REFUSAL

Guest-edited by
Jill Stoner and Ozayr Saloojee

06 | Vol 92 | 2022

ARCHITECTURES OF REFUSAL

About the Guest-Editors   5

Jill Stoner and Ozayr Saloojee

Introduction   6

Repair, Reworld

The Many Ways of Saying 'No'

Jill Stoner and Ozayr Saloojee

Prologue   14

Drawing an Argument for Refusal

Ozayr Saloojee

Centring Civilisation   22

Now and *After* the Apocalypse

Alberto de Salvatierra

Digital Doubles   30

The Major Agency of Minor Bits

Lucía Jalón Oyarzun

Expanding Bodies   38

Pedagogical Models for Pluralistic Spatialities

Quilian Riano

Shebeen Operations   46

Navigating Deviance

Thireshen Govender

Earth Versus FIFA   54

Resisting Globalisation on the Open Pitch

Hannah le Roux

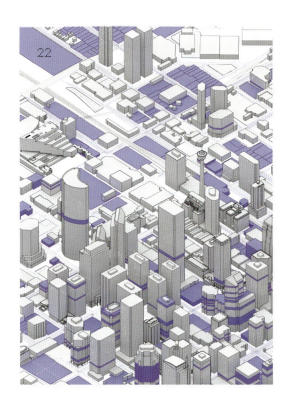

A Cottage to Breathe In   62

Refusing Museums, Making Homes

Ilze Wolff

A Space of Problems   68

The Child-Cities of Columbus

Jennifer Newsom and Tom Carruthers

ISSN 0003-8504   ISBN 978 1119 833963   Guest-edited by **Jill Stoner and Ozayr Saloojee**

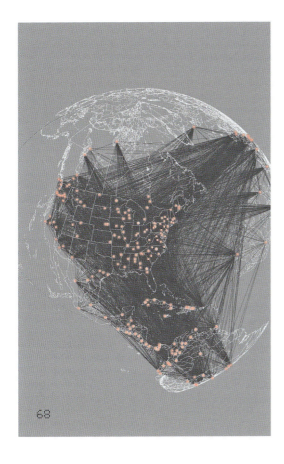

Reclaiming Their Future 78
Riotous Resistance and Indigenous Creativity in South America's Highest Metropolis

Carwil Bjork-James

The Eruv as Legal Fiction 86
Changing Rules in the Public Realm

Piper Bernbaum

From Altars to Alterity 94
Offerings and Inheritances for Queer Vietnamese Kin

Thompson Cong Nguyen

101 Ways to Refuse a Wall 102

Chat Travieso

Meanwhile Bodies 110
Architecture Without Property

Cathy Smith

To Not Refuse Our Ravaged World 120

Jill Stoner

'For decades, architecture has refused to acknowledge its contributions to social and environmental injustices, instead blithely perpetuating exploitative practices in the name of high art. But now, alternative practices and theorists across the world are refusing to comply.'

— Jill Stoner and Ozayr Saloojee

From Another Perspective

Balking in the Balkans 128
Lebbeus Woods – *Zagreb Free Zone* Revisited

Neil Spiller

Contributors 134

Editorial Offices
John Wiley & Sons
9600 Garsington Road
Oxford
OX4 2DQ

T +44 (0)18 6577 6868

Editor
Neil Spiller

Managing Editor
Caroline Ellerby
Caroline Ellerby Publishing

Freelance Contributing Editor
Abigail Grater

Publisher
Todd Green

Art Direction + Design
Christian Küsters
CHK Design

Production Editor
Elizabeth Gongde

Prepress
Artmedia, London

Printed in the United Kingdom
by Hobbs the Printers Ltd

Front cover
Design by Christian Küsters
CHK Design

Inside front cover
Cathy Smith,
Meanwhile Bodies, 2022.
© Cathy Smith

Page 1
Ozayr Saloojee, *Sinan's Sokollu Mehmet Paşa, Istanbul (1568)*, 'Drawing an Argument for Refusal' series, 2022.
© Ozayr Saloojee

EDITORIAL BOARD

Denise Bratton
Paul Brislin
Mark Burry
Helen Castle
Nigel Coates
Peter Cook
Kate Goodwin
Edwin Heathcote
Brian McGrath
Jayne Merkel
Peter Murray
Mark Robbins
Deborah Saunt
Patrik Schumacher
Ken Yeang

ARCHITECTURAL DESIGN
November/December
2022
Volume 92
Issue 06

Disclaimer
The Publisher and Editors cannot be held responsible for errors or any consequences arising from the use of information contained in this journal; the views and opinions expressed do not necessarily reflect those of the Publisher and Editors, neither does the publication of advertisements constitute any endorsement by the Publisher and Editors of the products advertised.

Journal Customer Services
For ordering information, claims and any enquiry concerning your journal subscription please go to www.wileycustomerhelp.com/ask or contact your nearest office.

Americas
E: cs-journals@wiley.com
T: +1 877 762 2974

Europe, Middle East and Africa
E: cs-journals@wiley.com
T: +44 (0)1865 778 315

Asia Pacific
E: cs-journals@wiley.com
T: +65 6511 8000

Japan (for Japanese-speaking support)
E: cs-japan@wiley.com
T: +65 6511 8010

Visit our Online Customer Help available in 7 languages at www.wileycustomerhelp.com/ask

Print ISSN: 0003-8504
Online ISSN: 1554-2769

Prices are for six issues and include postage and handling charges. Individual-rate subscriptions must be paid by personal cheque or credit card. Individual-rate subscriptions may not be resold or used as library copies.

All prices are subject to change without notice.

Identification Statement
Periodicals Postage paid at Rahway, NJ 07065. Air freight and mailing in the USA by Mercury Media Processing, 1850 Elizabeth Avenue, Suite C, Rahway, NJ 07065, USA.

USA Postmaster
Please send address changes to *Architectural Design*, John Wiley & Sons Inc., c/o The Sheridan Press, PO Box 465, Hanover, PA 17331, USA

Rights and Permissions
Requests to the Publisher should be addressed to:
Permissions Department
John Wiley & Sons Ltd
The Atrium
Southern Gate
Chichester
West Sussex PO19 8SQ
UK

F: +44 (0)1243 770 620
E: Permissions@wiley.com

All Rights Reserved. No part of this publication may be reproduced, stored in a retrieval system or transmitted in any form or by any means, electronic, mechanical, photocopying, recording, scanning or otherwise, except under the terms of the Copyright, Designs and Patents Act 1988 or under the terms of a licence issued by the Copyright Licensing Agency Ltd, 5th Floor, Shackleton House, Battle Bridge Lane, London SE1 2HX, without the permission in writing of the Publisher.

Subscribe to *D*
D is published bimonthly and is available to purchase on both a subscription basis and as individual volumes at the following prices.

Prices
Individual copies:
£29.99 / US$45.00
Individual issues on *D* App for iPad:
£9.99 / US$13.99
Mailing fees for print may apply

Annual Subscription Rates
Student: £97 / US$151
print only
Personal: £151 / US$236
print and iPad access
Institutional: £357 / US$666
online only
Institutional: £373 / US$695
print only
Institutional: £401 / US$748
print and online

6-issue subscription on *D* App for iPad:
£44.99 / US$64.99

ABOUT THE GUEST-EDITORS

JILL STONER AND OZAYR SALOOJEE

During their six years as academic colleagues, Jill Stoner and Ozayr Saloojee have discovered a shared and deep commitment to expanding architecture's mandate, and to questioning the long-accepted Western canons of the profession. Their collaboration draws upon their complementary networks across six continents, and represents intersections of grass-roots practices, academic experimentation in design studios, and theoretical positions that push the very boundaries of architecture's definitions. Their vision for introducing the theme of this issue began with a refusal to privilege a single work on the cover. In this shared project, they seek to trouble architectural convention in the contexts of common senses, familiar orientations, glib geographies, uncritical histories and modes of perception.

Jill Stoner is Professor at the Graduate School of the University of California, Berkeley, where she taught in the department of architecture for 28 years. She recently completed a term as Director of the Azrieli School of Architecture and Urbanism at Carleton University in Ottawa, Canada. With a first degree in literature, her work has consistently drawn evidence from both fiction and poetry, insights from outside the field that reveal architecture's problematic narrative. Her project Rubashov's House (1992) drew upon stories of solitary confinement to produce a solo exhibition at the Berkeley Art Museum. Her first book, *Poems for Architects* (William Stout Publishers, 2001) is an anthology of 48 poems that reveal transformations of spatial sensibility throughout the 20th century. A second book, *Toward a Minor Architecture* (MIT Press, 2012) unravels the myths of architecture's colonial history through literary references, and advocates for a more politicised approach to the built environment. Recent writings are focused towards broader audiences, weaving together themes of climate change, the corruption of language and lessons of companion species. Her recent essays 'The End of the Idea of Island' and 'Migrants with Wings' were published on Literary Hub.

Ozayr Saloojee is Associate Editor of Design for the *Journal of Architectural Education (JAE)*, faculty in architecture at Carleton University, where he is also cross-appointed at the Institute for African Studies and affiliate faculty at the Carleton Center for the Study of Islam. He received his BArch and post-professional MArch II (Theory + Culture) from Carleton, and his PhD from the Bartlett School of Architecture, University College London (UCL). He has been shortlisted twice to curate the Canadian Pavilion at the Venice Architecture Biennale, with the collectives Fluid Boundaries in 2018, and with HiLo/YOW+ in 2022. Born and raised in Johannesburg, South Africa, his teaching and creative practice focuses on the spatial implications of contested political landscapes, geo-imaginaries and design justice, and he maintains research interests in the art and architecture of the Islamic worlds. Recent publications include collaborative writings with Dr Zoe Todd and Émélie Desrochers-Turgeon theorising on the notion of the Kerosphere (University of Toronto Press) and 'Kerogenic relations' (*Transmediale*, 2022) to foreground ethical and recociliatory relations with land and kin. 𐊨

Text © 2022 John Wiley & Sons Ltd. Images: (t) © Ben Stoner-Duncan; (b) © Ozayr Saloojee

Daniel Effah,
The Shadow as an Episteme,
'Between This Space and Me:
Tracing the Shadow as an Episteme',
MArch thesis,
Carleton University, Ottawa,
2022

Using the Photoshop image manipulation tools of 'Dodge' and 'Burn', this image is a meditation on the shadow as an episteme, and its entanglements with racialisation, inequality and the built environment. The shadow becomes a world-building, world-knowing and world-seeking exercise of emancipatory visual and spatial practice, akin to the pole shadows cast by Dream The Combine's *Columbus Columbia Colombo Colón* installation, in Indiana (2021) – see pp 68–77.

REPAIR, REWORLD

THE MANY WAYS OF SAYING 'NO'

INTRODUCTION

JILL STONER AND
OZAYR SALOOJEE

We begin with three avatars of refusal. The first is Herman Melville's hapless anti-hero Bartleby, a scrivener who one day simply refuses to work.[1] 'I prefer not to' is his response when given his daily task by the narrator. Self-effacing and nearly mute, Bartleby embodies passive resistance taken to an extreme. Eventually, he refuses even to eat, and slowly wastes away.

In our own time, in 2018, a young schoolgirl in Sweden began by refusing to attend school, spending days holding up a simple sign as she sat on the public pavement: 'School Strike for Climate'. Her initial, relatively polite resistance quickly gained recognition, and the ensuing momentum progressively gave Greta Thunberg a public, international platform. 'How dare you!?' she famously challenged world leaders at the UN climate conference in 2019, after refusing to burn carbon on a flight from Stockholm to New York, and instead making her way across the Atlantic on a boat.[2]

But an even more exemplary voice for refusal may be Juliet's plea from the balcony: 'O Romeo, Romeo, wherefore art thou Romeo? / Deny thy father and refuse thy name.'[3] She is asking him, in refusing the Montague name, to honour his love for her over any social or familial obligations. Refusal here is much more than a symbolic spurn. It goes to the very core of authenticity, with absolute commitment and commitment's alter ego: risk.

REVERSING THE NATURE OF REFUSAL
In the 14th century, English usage of the word 'refuse' swerved towards the negative connotation of rejection and avoidance. But before that, the Vulgar Latin '*refusare*' was a direct descendant of the Proto Indo European root *gheu*, meaning 'to pour'. To refuse was to pour back, to flow back, to give back, to restore and return. There is nothing nostalgic here. In the domain of architecture, to return or flow again is simply to refuse all the calcifying, paralysing, limiting structures of patriarchal, colonial, binary spatial practices to which architecture has been held captive.

For decades, architecture has refused to acknowledge its contributions to social and environmental injustices, instead blithely perpetuating exploitative practices in the name of high art. But now, alternative practices and theorists across the world are refusing to comply. This issue is dedicated to some of those counter-refusals, critiquing a wide range of past canons and patterns that include privileging colonial ruling classes, exploiting labour, privatising public space and excluding of other species.

The opening article 'Drawing An Argument for Refusal' challenges the drawing convention of the analytique as a means of understanding the complex life of a building, through a drawing project that world-builds from the temporalities of architecture, history and the colonial sleight-of-hand of drafted lines and drawing conventions. Here, the practice of refusal is both method, memory and meaning, and a deliberate counter to the universalism of drawing practice. Here, drawings are not a ruse of knowing, but a reparative claiming of time, space and place, always from the so-called architectural centre of the Mediterranean world. This is a project of flowing back, with drawing as its fluid medium.

REDEFINING DEFINITIONS, REFUSING BOUNDARIES
Alberto de Salvatierra, in his piece 'Centring Civilisation: Now and *After* the Apocalypse', extends this un-centring to the scale of the civilisational, both in the politics of a name – at the Center for Civilization at the University of Calgary's School of Architecture, Planning and Landscape which he directs – and in the urgency of climate catastrophe. Drawing on the work of Bruno Latour, Vaclav Smil, Alexander von Humboldt and Design Earth, de Salvatierra argues for a refusal of 'skewed systems' and the reifying of a 'darker, techno-enabled totalitarian dystopia'.

Lucía Jalón Oyarzun shifts the scale of refusal to the minor and questions the (major) computational hegemony of Autodesk, IBM and Alphabet, arguing for the 'open repertoire of spatial practices and know-hows attentive to the differentiating agency of the real'. Oyarzun resists 'proprietary algorithms', in order to reach practices of the incomputable, the uncertain, and 'material fuzziness'. The minor, as a praxis of refusal, is a type of learning keyed to the no-mean-feat of survival.

Quilian Riano brings the practice of refusal to teaching through design studios in Canada and the US. With the improvisational work of landscape architect Walter J Hood and Brazilian theatre practitioner Augusto Boal's 'Theatre of the Oppressed' as conceptual frameworks, he asks students to challenge the very notion of the generic body. Riano, at Kent State College of Architecture and Environmental Design, and with Jenn Low (as a faculty teaching pair from the Dark Matter University) at Carleton University's Azrieli School of Architecture and Urbanism, explore – with students – the collaborative practice of design, challenging students to re-imagine subjectivity as intersectional bodies.

REFUSING THE COLONIAL
The following series of texts bring us to South Africa, and to the critical practice of architects and teachers Thireshen Govender and Hannah le Roux in Egoli (Johannesburg), and to the Mother City of Cape Town, through the work of Ilze Wolff of Wolff Architects. Govender's article explores deviance as refusal in the dynamic and sites of South African shebeens – drinking establishments that have significant agency as a formal and architectural typology to challenge static and still profoundly oppressive urban legal constraints. Shebeens, as agents of refusal and as commons of resistance, are investigated, documented, drawn and theorised as vital urban imaginaries.

From the pub to the soccer field. Hannah le Roux's text looks to the township football fields in the Witwatersrand region, and how football pitches serve as temporal claims to space in the *terrain vague* of buffer zones, and in response to the 2010 FIFA World Cup's failed promise of 'legacy projects' in Johannesburg's townships. Le Roux's 'open fields' serve as mediating agents upon the formal gesture of the white line drawn upon the earth to mark the extent of the field. They expose the power of appropriation, the refusals of 'enclosure, resurfacing … and exclusion', as she writes, to confront elites and to support community.

Ilze Wolff's article on the holiday home of Cecil John Rhodes – the British mining magnate and politician who served as the Prime Minister of the Cape Colony in the late 19th century – begins with an epigraph by South African author and freedom

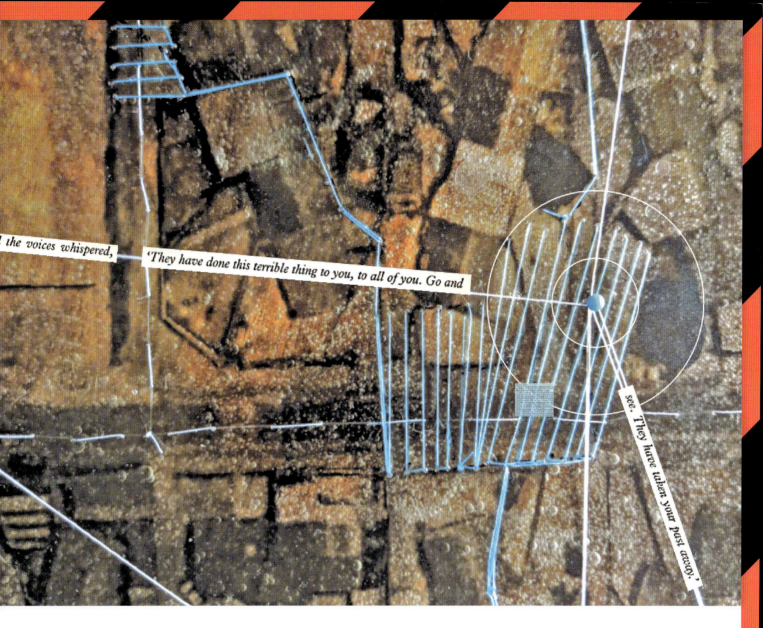

Gabrielle Argent,
Return to District Six, Cape Town,
'Mobility, Voice and View: Unpacking the Future of Cape Town's District Six',
MArch thesis, Carleton University, Ottawa,
2020

On the site of the old Cape Town called District Six, abandoned since its residents were banished to townships in the hinterlands, Argent's project imagines a return to this ground. It is refusal made visible through stories, and accessible through the design of a new aerial public transit system. Like the shebeens discussed in Thireshen Govender's article, the remaking of District Six is generated by narrative licence and ambiguous edges.

IN THE DOMAIN OF ARCHITECTURE, TO RETURN OR FLOW AGAIN IS SIMPLY TO REFUSE ALL THE CALCIFYING, PARALYSING, LIMITING STRUCTURES OF PATRIARCHAL, COLONIAL, BINARY SPATIAL PRACTICES TO WHICH ARCHITECTURE HAS BEEN HELD CAPTIVE

Rudo Mpisaunga,
A New Map of Zambia,
'Towing the Line: Unravelling and Reconstructing Identity Along the Zambezi River',
MArch thesis, Carleton University,
Ottawa,
2022

Picking up where Namwali Serpell's novel *The Old Drift* (2019) ends, this image is a speculation on a new map of Lusaka, following catastrophic infrastructural failure. It investigates new modalities of mapping and *placing*, as part of a local reckoning with colonial history and future possibility. Mpisaunga's drawing is seen here as an analogue to Wolff Architects' proposal to reconsider the Rhodes Cottage in Cape Town.

advocate Bessie Head, where she notes of Rhodes that 'You look across the land as a black person and you feel choked.' Here, Wolff connects back to Oyarzun's earlier piece and her citing of Frantz Fanon, bell hooks and the tragic death of Eric Garner. Her text reflects on Wolff Architects' conservation management plan, appointed through a public tender process by the City of Cape Town, to develop a site management, educational, research and conservation plan for the house of the man who noted in 1896 that 'I have taken everything from them but the air.'

The award-winning architectural practice Dream The Combine – led by Jennifer Newsom and Tom Carruthers – reflects on the local and global legacy of Christopher Columbus in the Midwest modern 'mecca of Columbus'. Their article explores his extractivist, genocidal legacy through an installation of vertical markers in Mill Race Park, Columbus, Indiana as a practice of attunement to the 'silences of loss' that connect us. Their work constructs a spatial imaginary of the so-called city-on-a-hill. Etched with narratives from other places named after the same man, and laid out through Mercator projections, this is an architecture of discursive refusal and of accountability.

(NEARLY) INVISIBLE LINES OF REFUSAL
Piper Bernbaum's piece on the Jewish eruv complements these narratives of contemporary spatial politics with a practice that is centuries old. Essentially, eruvin (plural) refuse the conventional definition of domestic territory, as a way of negotiating between Orthodox Sabbath law and the necessities of daily life. As a barely visible line through neighbourhoods around the world, the eruv serves as a model for subtle resistances that define space without occupying it.

Carwil Bjork-James's study of recent urban developments in Bolivia brings to light a lesser-known case of indigenous leadership and of collective resistance to colonial assumptions about hierarchy, infrastructure and convention. It is the most 'active' example of refusal in this collection, as both a violent deconstruction of a former transit system and a political tour de force of innovative replacement: the *teleferico*.

```
Kirsten Larson,
Roda de Samba,
São Paulo, Brazil,
'City of Bridges: Performative
Urbanisms of the Everyday',
MArch thesis,
University of California,
Berkeley,
2015
```

Larson's proposal for a bridge in São Paulo traces in dynamic lines and patterns an architecture that refuses substance in favour of motion. Instead of walls, the beating of *cuicos*, the engagement with *butecos*, the dizzying choreography of *sambistas* on a typical Sunday, as 'meanwhile' as the bodies in Cathy Smith's article.

RULES OF REFUSAL

The next cluster of three articles are entangled with the knotty problems of rules, identity and property. The artist, urbanist and designer Chat Travieso confronts the notion of refusal by removal – which becomes part of the lexicon in his piece where he argues for strategies of strategic disregard, appropriation, circumvention and abolition in aid of ethical architectural futures, noting: 'If architecture is a form of regulation, its refusal is a form of civil disobedience.'

MArch graduate Thompson Cong Nguyen explores the construction of alterior bodies through the architecture of offering for queer Vietnamese kin, in the shape of three altars designed at the scale of the room, the street and the club. Nguyen aims, as he writes, to 'develop a spatial practice that deeply considers the dimensional tolerances and (in)visible infrastructures as well as the shared joy and loss of my community and family.'

Architect and educator Cathy Smith extends this refusal into the needs of 'meanwhile bodies' and their tenuous relationships with the built environment. Like Travieso's strategies for refusal, for Smith, the precarity of the 'meanwhile body' shows the tension of positive images of, in her words, 'tactical urbanism, artisanal and creative enterprise, and "pop-up" retail', in contrast to the lived world of 'indeterminate accommodation'. How can the nomadic's embrace of otherness through feminist, post-structuralist and post-humanist discourse enable new spaces, types and figurations?

The final article, 'To Not Refuse a Ravaged World', reminds us that we must face forward, acknowledging all we have already built, and by building, all that we have obliterated. This is our context. In refusing architecture's exhausted and destructive spatial myths – of tabula rasa, wasted resources, anthropocentrism, boundaries, award-winning objects, heroic achievements, binary exclusions, permanence and growth – we accept the ravaged world we have made, as we have made it, as our point of departure. Feminist philosopher Donna Haraway calls it 'staying with the trouble'.[4] Geographer AM Kanngieser calls it 'refusal as return',[5] which returns us to the very root of refusal – a 'pouring back' into the vessel of a ravaged landscape of all that we feel and care about, recognising architecture not as a noun but as a verb, defined by action, perpetually unfinished and messily contingent.

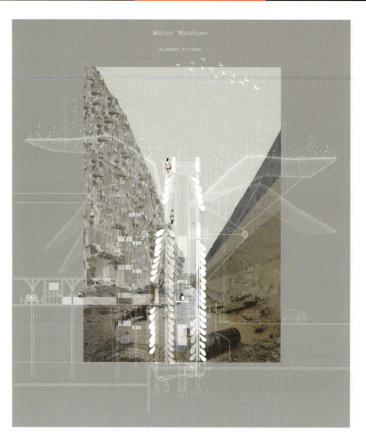

Ozayr Saloojee,
Maqluba, Olive, Watermelon (fragment),
'Street/Food' series, 2021

The image is a fragment of a drawing on food as resistance and refusal in Palestine. Here, textures of olives, watermelons and a traditional Palestinian dish *(maqluba)* become part of a constantly fragmenting and re-assembling map of Palestinian pasts, through a drawing practice that riffs on the Vitruvian Man and Le Corbusier's Modulor – as Quilian Riano writes about in his article in this issue.

Maya Jarrah,
Water Machine,
Aleppo, Syria,
'Against Gravity', MArch thesis,
Carleton University, Ottawa,
2020

opposite: The Water Machine, part of Jarrah's MArch thesis, is inspired by the historic public water taps, basins and fountains that existed in the city for hundreds of years. The machines, operated and enjoyed by the local community as they rebuild, act as infrastructure for capturing and filtering rainwater through large 'wings' that are mechanically spread when heavy rain pours over the city. These are 'meanwhile' structures, whose lifespans are undetermined and flexible.

REFUSAL IN THIS TIME OF WAR

In the first days of the invasion of Ukraine, a Ukrainian woman boldly offered a handful of sunflower seeds to a Russian soldier, saying: 'Take these seeds and put them in your pockets, so at least sunflowers will grow when you all lie down here.'[6]

The production of this issue is concurrent with the war on Ukraine, and our oversaturated media leave little to be imagined of its ravaged landscape. Ukrainian cities manifested traditions of European styles, symbols and hierarchies overlaid with a more recent proliferation of Soviet expediency. So the war also reveals a paradox: the Ukrainian people's refusal to succumb to tyranny has gained massive support from the very nations that are responsible for Western architecture's spatial tyrannies. All manner of nations and individual architects have offered to plan whole cities, or to reproduce significant buildings. But the question of how to rebuild these cities cannot be about replacing what has been destroyed. Here is an opportunity to continue to watch and listen to the Ukrainian people, as they weave camouflage nets out of scraps of cloth, repurpose building fragments as roadblocks, broadcast sunflower seeds onto the contaminated ground. Ukrainian President Volodymyr Zelenskyy refused an easy exit strategy offered by the US, of an escape out of Kyiv. He elected, rather, to stay and asked instead for ammunition. While the stakes may be less immediate and obvious here, in an issue of ⌓, the questions and issues raised herein are life-risking all the same – and particularly for communities who have been systematically and historically excluded, disenfranchised, marginalised, othered and refused.

This issue of ⌓ – which refused the tradition of a single lionised image on its cover and the privileging, therefore, of a single unitary work – looks to refusal also as hope, permission, and care – like sunflowers growing in a field. ⌓

NOTES
1. Herman Melville, *Bartleby, the Scrivener: A Story of Wall Street*, Simon & Schuster (New York), 1997.
2. Anne Barnard, 'Greta Thunberg, Climate Activist, Arrives in NY with a Message for Trump', *New York Times*, 25 September 2019: www.nytimes.com/2019/08/28/nyregion/greta-thunberg-new-york.html.
3. William Shakespeare, *Romeo and Juliet*, Act 2, Scene 1, lines 74–6.
4. Donna Haraway, *Staying With the Trouble: Making Kin in the Chthulucene*, Duke University Press (Durham, NC), 2016.
5. AM Kanngieser, 'To Undo Nature; On Refusal as Return', *Transmediale*, 2021: https://amkanngieser.com/work/to-undo-nature-on-refusal-as-return.
6. Shweta Sharma, 'Brave Ukrainian Woman Tells Russian Soldier: "Put Sunflower Seeds In Your Pocket So They Grow When You Die"', *Independent*, 25 February 2022: www.independent.co.uk/news/world/europe/ukraine-russia-soldier-woman-confrontation-b2022993.html.

Jill Stoner,
Sunflower, Ottawa,
2020

The French word for sunflower is *tournesol*, which might be translated as 'turn (to) sun'. This perfectly describes the plant's heliotropic nature, facing east each morning and rotating towards the west like a sundial's shadow. It is both rooted and mobile, a fitting vegetal mascot for an ethics of refusal.

Text © 2022 John Wiley & Sons Ltd. Images: p 6 © Daniel Effah; p 9 © Gabrielle Argent; p 10 © Rudo Mpisaunga; p 11 © Kirsten Larson; p 12 (t) © Maya Jarrah; p 12(b) © Ozayr Saloojee; p 13 © Jill Stoner

Ozayr Saloojee

PROLOGUE

DRAWING AN ARGU

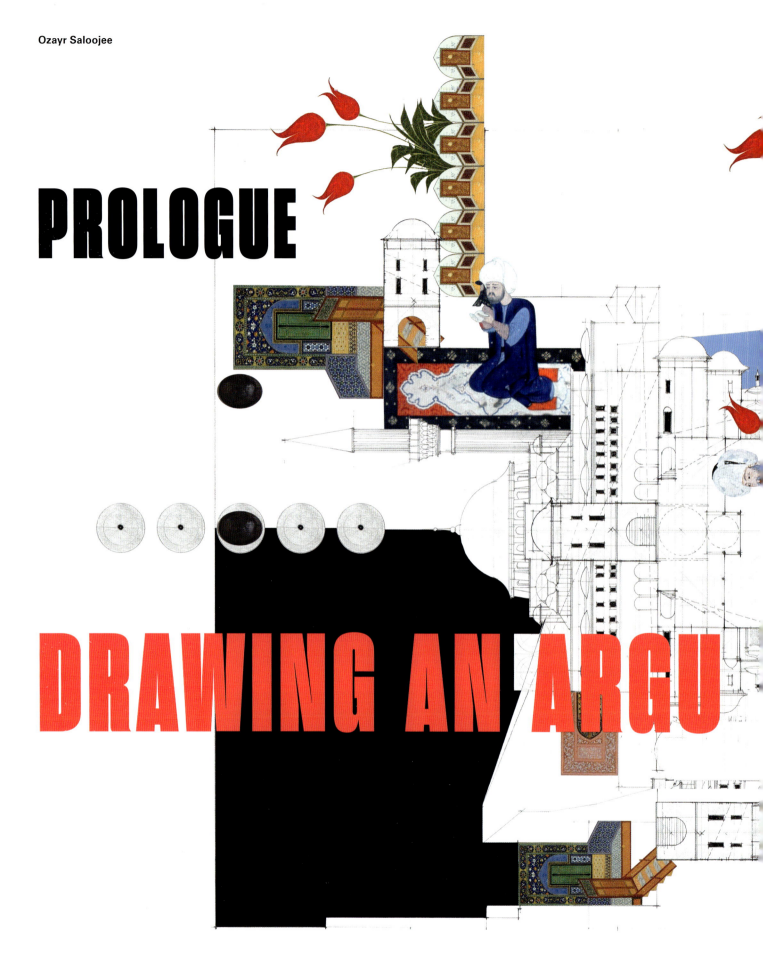

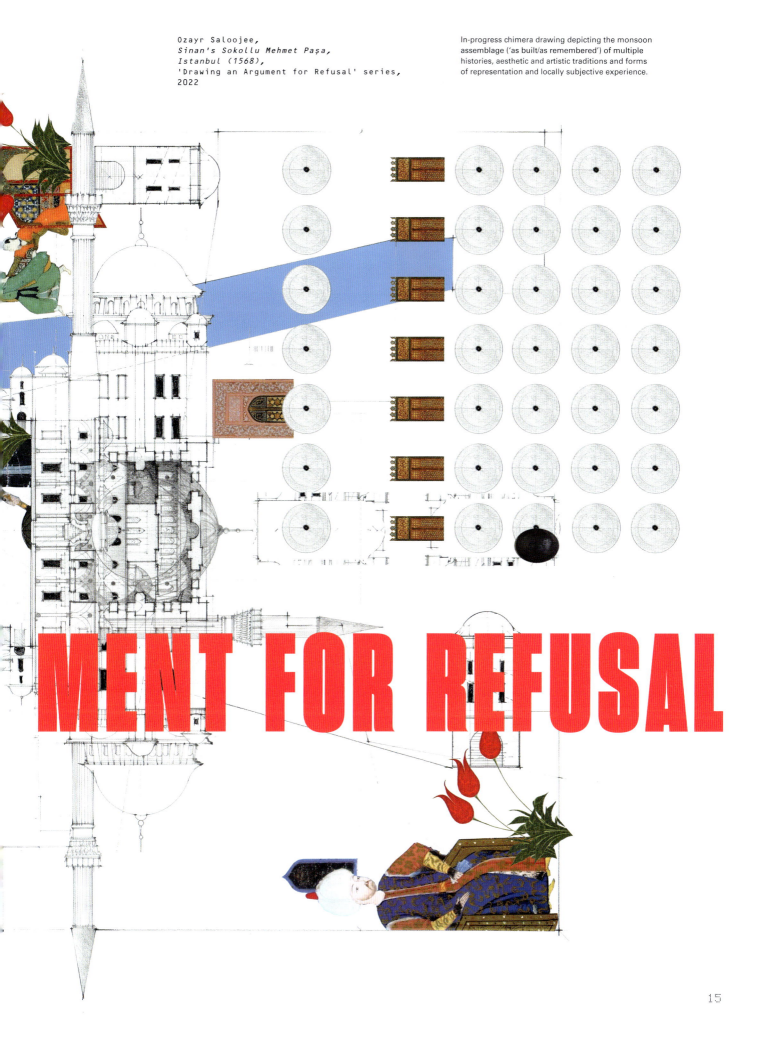

Ozayr Saloojee,
Sinan's Sokollu Mehmet Paşa, Istanbul (1568),
'Drawing an Argument for Refusal' series, 2022

In-progress chimera drawing depicting the monsoon assemblage ('as built/as remembered') of multiple histories, aesthetic and artistic traditions and forms of representation and locally subjective experience.

The way an architectural drawing is composed and formatted is underwritten by its reliance on Western, modernist protocols of space-making and construction. Guest-editor of this issue and faculty in architecture at Carleton University in Ottawa, Ozayr Saloojee describes his drawing practice as a way to destabilise these assumptions and introduce in his work more social and political issues not prevalent in the western cannon.

The Mississippi River, Minneapolis, Minnesota, 2016

The Mississippi River at sunset, seen from Interstate 94.

Instead of graphite (2B lead) and paper (Strathmore, 2-ply); instead of a line drawn with the edge of a 45-degree triangle on a Borco-lined 3 x 4 foot table with its Mayline rule, I begin with a river. Rather than a drawing convention, I choose a liquid landscape.

Pick a river. Any river. Pick the Pasapkedjinawong if you are in Odawa/Ottawa (where I am), or the Kaniatarowanenneh (the St Lawrence) if you happen to be in Tiohti:áke/Montreal, or the Kızılırmak (the Red River) if you are in Cappadocia. Perhaps the Mississippi if you are in Minneapolis? Or maybe you are in Davenport, or St Louis or Memphis, or at the Mississippi's so-called 'end' where it bleeds out beyond New Orleans and empties its fluvial deposition of sands, silts and clays into the Delta, out into the Gulf of Mexico.

Let me begin drawing an argument for refusal through a riverine thought by Professor Dilip da Cunha, where he asks: 'Are rivers products of a visual literacy – the literacy of the drawn line separating land from water – before they are natural entities that they are believed to be? Does this literacy privilege a moment in time when water is not precipitating, seeping, soaking air, soil and vegetation, collecting, evaporating, and transpiring in ways that defy delineation?'[1]

So. Not a river then. A basin? A watershed? Insufficient, as these are still constructs of hydrologic science, and anthropocentric projections of rarified cartographies onto the ubiquitous wetness of aqua fluxis. These are still the meanings, knowledges and values of terra firma, of land-locked and terrestrial framings of everything – including things which are not land. Everything is swept up into a limited geopoetics of earth and lithic constraint.[2]

In professor and author Karen Coelho's Foreword to the book *Monsoon as Method: Assembling Monsoonal Multiplicities* (2002), and of thinking with the monsoon as a mode of knowing, she cites feminist scholar and philosopher Karen Barad's 'thesis that our practices of knowledge-making are not outside of the phenomena we describe'.[3] So, not only a riverine line/river/basin/watershed, but a cycle, a continuum, a rain terrain. What is the seeping, soaking, evaporating, cycling, drizzling, oozing 'monsoon assemblage'[4] of reading and knowing a place, a body, a drawing, and therefore a world? Rather than outside a world, we begin within it. Rather than parts, we look to the whole and ask what is a drawing as a natural entity that is not circumscribed by a visual literacy?[5]

BODY: ARGUMENT
'Drawing an Argument for Refusal' is a meditation on thinking-through, destabilising and transforming the architectural drawing convention of the 'analytique' (a Beaux-Arts architectural drawing exercise) to develop a practice of knowledge-making as interior to the phenomena it describes. In *The Wretched of the Earth* (1961), Frantz Fanon writes of the poisoning, infecting and devaluing of the customs, traditions and the 'myths, especially their myths'[6] of the colonised when they come into contact with the coloniser. 'Drawing an Argument

for Refusal' is a project that explores an architectural mythos of seeing and knowing through a refusal of the epistemological and ontological structure of the analytique, a drawing described by architect and theorist Marco Frascari as an attempt to 'single out the dialogue among the parts in the making of a building'.[7] The project refuses Frascari's univocal conversation ('the dialogue'), refuses the cartesian bifurcation of fragments ('the parts') and refuses the order problem of the analytique ('the building') as a way to know worlds outside of the Académie Royal d'Architecture, the Académie des Beaux-Arts and their global pedagogical lineages and consequences.

The analytique practice was embedded in North American pedagogy during the early 20th century at the University of Pennsylvania, through the efforts of John Harbeson, Lloyd Warren and Paul Phillipe Cret, and through the work of other eager proponents such as Constant Despradelles at the Massachusetts Institute of Technology (MIT), Maurice J Prevot at Cornell University and more.[8] 'Drawing an Argument for Refusal' troubles the analytique as a pedagogical tool of teaching and learning, as a device that occludes the experience of worlds and architectures outside the intellectual orbit of Eurocentric paradigms. It problematises its unitary model of Western modernity, and argues that the analytique's universal sameness forecloses *other* possibilities of world-building and world-knowing. The analytique itself refuses this through the very structure of its deployment as a drawing exercise in Beaux-Arts pedagogy. It is framed through a very prescriptive sequence: (1) Esquisse, (2) Preparation for the First Criticism, and laying out the schedule, (3) Studying the Problem, (4) The Use of Documents, (5) Composing the Sheet, (6) Passing to Ink, (7) Rendering, and (8) Rendering, concluded. It results in drawings 'as built/as known'. It emphasises sequence, linearity, empirical relations, and as a result a closed and internal theoretical loop. 'Drawing an Argument for Refusal', however, looks to drawings 'as remembered/as (im)possible', emphasising the meta-spatial, the nonlinear, the embodied, the open work, the locally subjective and relational ecologies.

Where the analytique centres the fragment in a composition, this project refuses to acknowledge the notion of a fragment at all. It refuses the Cartesian bifurcation of the analytique, of singly its sources and worlds (for example, knowing and seeing the architecture of Egypt *only* with the works of the late 19th- and early 20th-century architect, conservator and historian Max Herz, Napoleon's *Description De L'Egypte* (1809–1929) and the early 20th-century English architectural historian Sir Archibald Cresswell's drawings). The refusal drawings instead propose a conciliatory and reparative framing of what have been seen as unusable pasts as *usably* present, future seeking and world-grounded. They offer a visual (il)literacy as built *and* as remembered, and of refusal as a mode of (un)knowing to generate emancipatory historiographies.

CODA: DRAWING

At last, to graphite and paper. The drawings are a counter to the analytique and 'world-seek' and 'world-affirm' through a set of three buildings each in Istanbul, Cairo, Rome, Fez and Spain, all of which are considered sites of historic Eurocentric 'expertise' and 'authority'. As a drawing project, they question the so-called historicities and universal interpretations of what are ultimately local subjectivities and local worlds, and how these terrains have been 'enworlded' as an intellectual project, and professionalised by a body of research that has, for much of the long march of architectural teaching, been the purview of those outside of local customs, traditions and myths.

The drawings were prompted by the pandemic shutdown of 2020. Motivated in part by the closing of a privileged world of travel, by frustration and worry over vaccines and illness, the project began as a response to the denial of movement: a need to try to keep busy and to find an internal, reflective and critical practice of diving back into a wellspring of memory. It became, over a period of the two years since my last flight (returning from teaching a drawing workshop in Andalucía in March 2020), a way to return to many homes, experienced since the first related trip abroad to visit one of these sites (Egypt, 1999), to the most recent trip to Spain in 2020. An ongoing project, 'Drawing An Argument for Refusal' has become a meditation on 23 years of landscape encounter. The three buildings selected for each site were drawn, incrementally, over the first summer of the Covid-19 pandemic. Constraints were set: graphite only (a range of 2-millimetre leads), Strathmore 2-ply paper and drafting dots. All places were sites I had visited, documented or drawn in some way, were meaningful to me personally, and were sites of gathering with at least one courtyard. Fifteen drawings took 16 weeks, and each began with unfolding the elevations around central building courtyards. The Sokollu Mehmet Paşa drawing (the first in the series) has one courtyard; the last drawing (the Réal Alcazar in Seville) has more than 10.

WHERE THE ANALYTIQUE CENTRES THE FRAGMENT IN A COMPOSITION, THIS PROJECT REFUSES TO ACKNOWLEDGE THE NOTION OF A FRAGMENT AT ALL

Growing outward from their courtyard cores, the drawings were constructed around the overlaps of flattened façades over drafted architectural plans. The Istanbul drawings were the simplest of all; I was finding my footing on an unsteady ground. The Rome drawings celebrate the *pochér*, inspired by Giambattista Nolli and his plan for Rome (1748). The Cairo drawings celebrate patterns, and the Fez drawings are sky-attentive, textural, and embody a history of intense travel experience. The Andalucían drawings are chimeras of Islamic history and Reconquista narratives. As the project unfolded, writing became a core component of telling the story of these 'as remembered/as (im)possible worlds', reconstructed from memory and my own photographic archives and documents. The poetry of Ibn Zamrak (1333–93) – a court poet of the Alhambra – became a corollary to the Nasrid Palace drawing. The words of the poet Muhammad Iqbal (1877–1938), meditating on the Guadalquivir river, were an accompaniment to the drawing of La Mezquita in Cordoba.

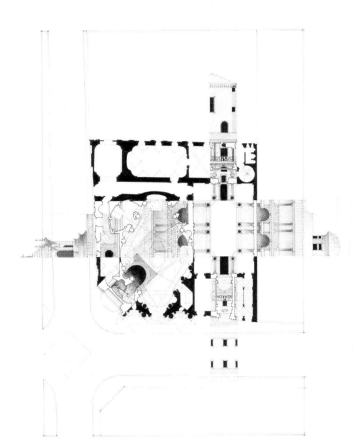

Ozayr Saloojee,
Francesco Borromini's San Carlo alle Quattro Fontane,
Rome (1638),
'Drawing an Argument for Refusal' series,
2022

above: Inspired by the Giambattista Nolli (1748) and Leonardo Buffalini (1551) maps of Rome, the drawing uses the *pochér* as a localised strategy of countering the typical analytique, along with Borromini's geometrical prowess.

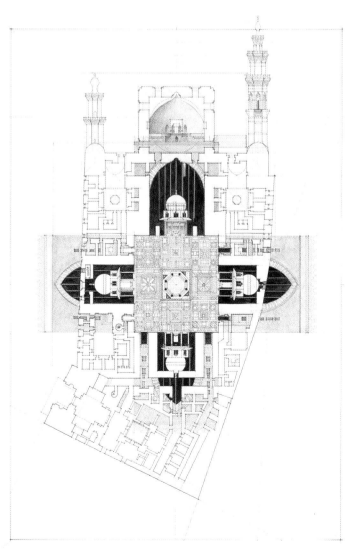

Ozayr Saloojee,
Muhammad ibn Biylik al-Muhsini's Sultan Hassan Mosque and Madrasa,
Cairo (1363),
'Drawing an Argument for Refusal' series,
2022

right: The supra-rational context of the geometric floor and its relation to Islamic spirituality and practice.

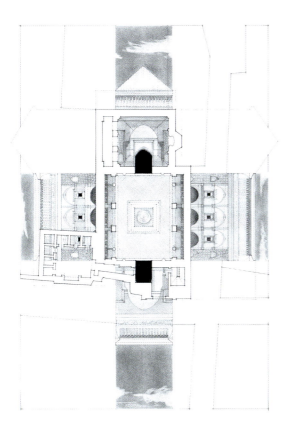

GROWING OUTWARD FROM THEIR COURTYARD CORES, THE DRAWINGS WERE CONSTRUCTED AROUND THE OVERLAPS OF FLATTENED FAÇADES OVER DRAFTED ARCHITECTURAL PLANS

Ozayr Saloojee,
Al'Attarine Madrasa,
Fez (1325),
'Drawing an Argument for Refusal' series,
2022

above: Drawing acknowledging the courtyard, commissioned by the Moroccan Sultan Abu Sa'id Uthman II, as a sky-framing device, and the building's texture, reflecting on the ceramic tile art of 'taqshir' – peeling away matte surface glazes to reveal glossy colour.

Ozayr Saloojee,
Alcazar of Seville (10th-14th centuries),
'Drawing an Argument for Refusal' series,
2022

right: The historical courts of the Royal Palace in Seville, including its Roman, Andalucian and Renaissance contexts. Known variously as the Royal Palace and (in Arabic) the Verdant Palace, the drawing explores palimpsest ideas of memory and forgetting in both Moorish and Reconquista narratives.

Ozayr Saloojee,
*Sinan's Sokollu Mehmet Paşa,
Istanbul (1568),*
'Drawing an Argument for Refusal' series,
2022

opposite, top left: Template for a crowd-sourced drawing that will build a version of the Sokollu Mehmet Paşa mosque as crafted and constructed by a process of collective (and non-expert) drawing inputs.

opposite, bottom right: The Sokollu Mehmet Paşa mosque is one of Sinan's finest works, and a brilliant urban response to a very complex, sloping site in the old city of Sultanahmet. Base drawing by research assistants Robert Oleksiak and Stuart Thompson with Ozayr Saloojee.

The Bosphorus,
Istanbul,
2020

The historic peninsula of Istanbul, seen from a commuter ferry from the Asian side of the city. The camera looks towards the Sokollu Mehmet Paşa mosque, out of frame behind the mass of the historic urban fabric in silhouette.

Each base drawing is part of a family of five and includes an accompanying text, a conventional site plan, a crowd-sourced drawing and a final chimera drawing. In the chimera drawing of the Sokollu Mehmet Paşa in Istanbul, the architect Sinan (*c* 1488–1588), Sultan Süleyman the Magnificent (1494–1566), and Joseph – an Islamic embodiment of beauty and character, chased by Zuleykha (Potiphar's wife) – are part of the unfolded scene of Sinan's mosque. Architectural components of the mosque are repeated and layered into the drawing, along with Ottoman and Persian miniature contexts. The ubiquitous Turkish tulip blooms across the page, and the *Hajar al-Aswad* – the sacred black stone that anchors the Ka'aba in Mecca – is present, reflecting its fragments that are present in the physical architecture of the mosque. While the drawing might offer visual resonance for some, its readings may be inaccessible – illegible even – to those not familiar with Joseph, Zuleykha, Sinan, Süleyman or the Black Stone. These drawings collapse (my) worlds and times, my geographies (real, lived and desired), and my myths, histories and counter-histories. These are not lines, but vectors, a monsoonal, visual illiteracy to counter the gate-keeping that kept the fullness of my world away from me. So, in the end, I do not choose a river. I choose the episteme of the Strait – the Bosphorus – with its multiple waters, continents, histories.

But this is a part of drawing an argument for refusal. Refusal is not only rejection, but possible inaccessibility. It might be denial for you, but it is permission for me. These drawings are monsoon assemblages. They are a visual illiteracy to protect and repair my architectural worlds, not necessarily yours; my memories, not necessarily yours; my pedagogy, not the Beaux-Arts; my (and for others like me) drawing, not theirs. I do not choose a border drawn by others to tell me how my world is circumscribed. I draw, rather, a refusal.

Not everything belongs to everyone. Drawing an argument for refusal is a way to reconstitute and reclaim myths, especially my myths, and not another's version of my histories and pasts, nor another's framing of my present and future. ⌂

Notes
1. Dilip Da Cunha, 'River Literacy and the Challenge of a Rain Terrain', *Journal of Contemporary Thought*, 41, Summer 2015, p 192.
2. See Aya Nassar, 'Geopoetics as Disruptive Aesthetics: Vignettes from Cairo', *GeoHumanities*, 7 (2), 2021, pp 455–63.
3. Karen Coelho, Foreword, in *Monsoon as Method: Assembling Monsoonal Multiplicities*, Actar (Barcelona), 2002, p 8.
4. See http://exhibition.monass.org/ for a full description of the Monsoon Assemblages research project.
5. See Vivek Dhareshwar, 'Sites of Learning and Intellectual Parasitism', *Journal of Contemporary Thought*, 41, Summer 2015, p 57.
6. Frantz Fanon, *The Wretched of the Earth* [1961], Grove Press (New York), 2004, p 7.
7. Marco Frascari, 'The Tell-The-Tale Detail', in JN Keely and MD Lenhart (eds), *Semiotics*, Springer (Boston, MA), 1981, p 24.
8. John F Harbeson, *The Study of Architectural Design*, WW Norton (New York), 2008.

Text © 2022 John Wiley & Sons Ltd.
Images © Ozayr Saloojee

Alberto de Salvatierra

Centring Civilisation

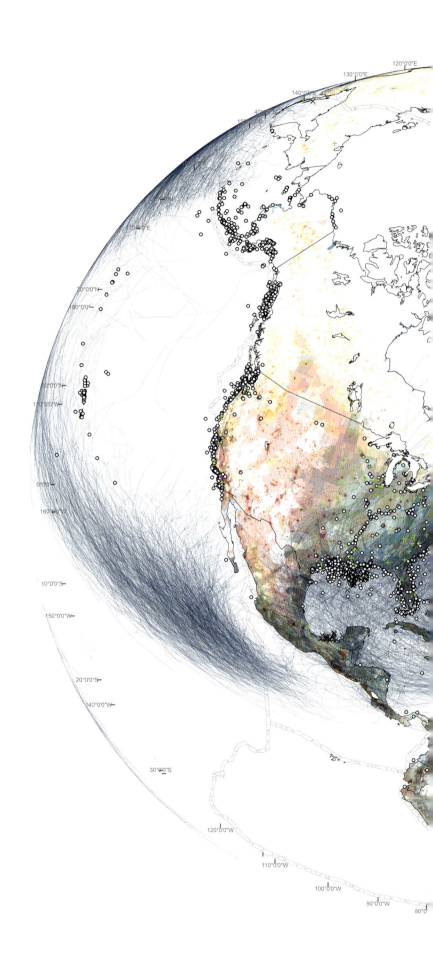

Alberto de Salvatierra and Tripty Kaur / Center for Civilization, Climate + Catastrophe: Mapping Global Landscapes of Crisis and Risk, 2022

Apocalypse map: Canada. Geospatial visualisation including mappings of risk across multiple categories (earthquakes, hurricanes, drought, sea-level rise, volcanic eruptions, oil spills, nuclear reactors).

Now and After the Apocalypse

The intersection of cities, bodies and politics and their material flows creates an interdisciplinary platform for new radical urbanisms. Alberto de Salvatierra, founder and director of the Center for Civilization and assistant professor of urbanism and data in architecture at the University of Calgary in Alberta, Canada, believes we are at a critical perturbation in human society, that all that has been stable for some time is now changing, more voices are being heard, and one dominant point of view is no longer predicated.

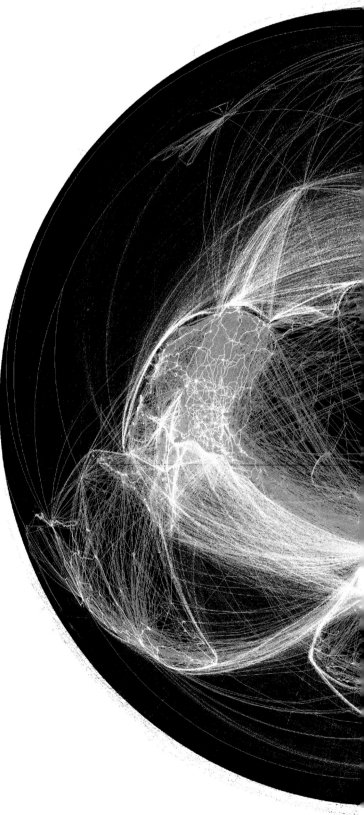

Alberto de Salvatierra / Center for Civilization, Weak Signals + Wild Cards: Agricultural Flows as Urbanisation in the Canadian Prairies, 2016

> Science is not enough, religion is not enough, art is not enough, politics and economics are not enough, nor is love, nor is duty, nor is action however disinterested, nor, however sublime, is contemplation. Nothing short of everything will really do.
> – Aldous Huxley, *Island*, 1962[1]

Civilisation as we know it is ending. Modern society, whether it knows it or not, has crossed a critical inflection point and now finds itself in the ambiguous, uncertain and indeterminate liminal space between 'how things "used" to be' and 'how things *will* be'. However, this ending is less of a terminus and more of a wind-down. Our current human chapter that began with the genocide of the Americas and the birth of trans-oceanic Empire was a project of establishing false centrings; it can no longer masquerade as a civilised world. But this 'civilisation' – ending, in an apocalypse no less – is a *fake* Civilisation, only a small portion of the *actual* Civilisation that a largely heteronormative, patriarchal, Eurocentric, white-supremacist and colonial-borne society has subjugated, displaced and ignored[2] in favour of a shadow of itself: the 'civilisation' used to 'elevate' the poor, unfortunate, non-European and non-Judaeo-Christian masses out of 'barbarism'. Within this context, how we exit our current chapter, and begin the next, will have the most severe consequences for our collective planetary tenure, positive or negative. An answer, or more appropriately the beginning of an answer, lies in a collective project of Civilisation. This is why we must centre it now – and *after* – the apocalypse.

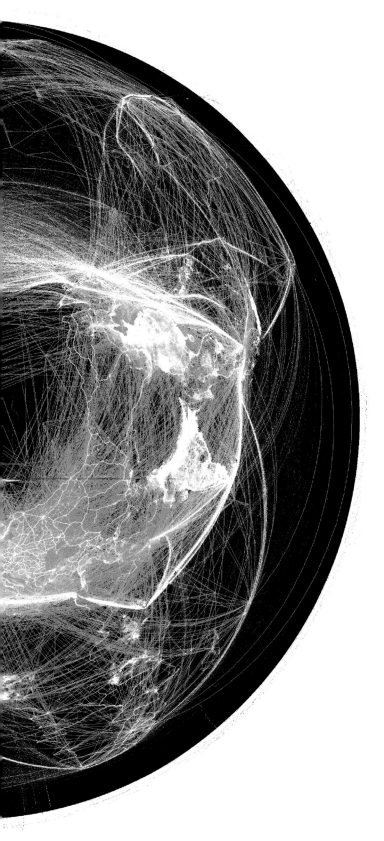

Global gradients of entropy map, from a research project focusing on how global material flows (particularly agricultural imports and exports) will influence urbanisation in the Canadian Prairies. The Earth is reconceived as a planetary system of material flows and infrastructure (roads and railways, shipping lanes, air routes) that begins to highlight the densities of human activity.

The Politics of a Name

The Center for Civilization at the University of Calgary School of Architecture, Planning and Landscape is a design research lab and international think tank working at the intersection of cities, society and civilisation. At first glance, the name evokes the most egomaniacal and narcissistic impulses of the architecture and design disciplines. And certainly, as a brown, queer person, I suspect my 'audacity' to name a lab as such would be much less pronounced if I were a different colour, came up and through a different socio-economic background, or if I more appropriately fitted into the spaces not made for people like me. Nevertheless, a quiet or overt indignation for an organisation so named remains. And tellingly, such reactions themselves reflect the context in which the word 'civilisation' has been brought up. The hierarchical and scalar associations of the words in the name alone ('centre' and 'civilisation') suggest some grand self-importance. The negative connotations, particularly around the historical genealogy of 'civilising', have been earned through blood and death. Yet the name 'Center for Civilization' speaks not and refers not to the prevailing Western-centric etymology; it encodes altogether different values.

First, 'Civilization' refers not to our (predominantly Eurocentric) 'civilisation', the manufactured fiction of our current *fake* Civilisation, but to the collective, pluralistic, syncretic construct of the *entirety* of 'human social and cultural development and organisation'.[3] This means that our current, prevailing 'civilisation', most recently distilled into its own geological epoch – the Anthropocene – is not one that should be recognised as Civilisation, for it often excludes black, brown and indigenous bodies, communities and practices.[4] As Bruno Latour writes in the closing chapter of his book *Down to Earth: Politics in the New Climatic Regime* (2018), 'Among these crimes there is, most important of all, the crime of having believed [Europe] could install itself in places, territories, countries, cultures in which it was necessary either to eliminate the inhabitants or to replace their forms of life by its own – in the name of an obligatory "civilisation". It is the crime, as we know, that enabled the image and the scientific form of the Globe.'[5] This image and this form, forged by a few and upheld as the reality of the many, is therefore fictional.[6] And, as a result, 'civilisation' is a word that has been widely co-opted by supremacy and colonialism. It is not this incorrect usage that should be enshrined, but rather the pluralistic version that should have never been the opening salvo used to enslave and murder continents.

Second, 'Center' refers to the act of finding balance, not the noun describing a privileged position. In fact, any physical location described as 'a centre' of Civilisation is a contradiction, no matter the scale – whether a city (eg Babylon), a country (eg 'merica!) or a continent (eg Europe). Civilisation (uppercase C), made up of *many* civilisations (lowercase c), is multi-nodal – a rich and variegated field distributed across the planet. So, 'Center for Civilization' is more of a mantra, a belief – an action – that humanity must find balance ('centredness') amongst

Alberto de Salvatierra /
Center for Civilization,
Eternal Ephemera: Soft
Infrastructures in the
Floating City of Uros,
Lake Titicaca, Peru,
2016

right: Uros Khantati island – just one of over a hundred floating islands that make up the city of Uros. The Eternal Ephemera project examined the reed architectures of Lake Titicaca's Uru people.

below: Axonometric, in collaboration with Anagha Patil (2021), showing the sectional profile of a single Uru island – Uros Khantati.

opposite: 'Eddy' fishing in the middle of his family's island, and surrounded by the totora reed constructions of its architecture.

the pluralistic and diverse constituencies that make up Civilisation, not a call to find the one to rule them all. One such project – Eternal Ephemera: Soft Infrastructures in the Floating City of Uros, Peru (2016–21) – examined the reed architectures of the Uru people of Lake Titicaca. How would humanity have differed in its development and trajectory towards our current climate collapse if only it had more seriously incorporated wisdoms of indigenous land stewardship, for example? For one, Uros, an ephemeral floating city made entirely out of woven reed islands, lives in harmony with its local ecology. As a civilisation, the Uru predate the Incas despite having had no solid monuments and being semi-nomadic.[7] Yet, after more than a millennium that saw them overcome attempts of conquest and assimilation, they are now threatened by climate change that is destabilising their native landscapes and economic forces that have promoted a consumerist-centric lifestyle, causing younger generations to abandon their cultural heritage in favour of a Western-imposed modernity.[8]

With new definitions in hand, we can proceed to answer the question, 'Why Civilisation?' and why we must 'centre' it now – and *after* – the apocalypse

The Project of Civilisation

With new definitions in hand, we can proceed to answer the question, 'Why Civilisation?' and why we must 'centre' it now – and *after* – the apocalypse. In short, the answer is climate change – the climax of our frenzied regimes of extraction. As Vaclav Smil, a Czech-Canadian scientist and policy analyst, writes: 'Modern civilization depends on extracting prodigious energy stores, depleting finite fossil fuel deposits that cannot be replenished even on time scales orders of magnitude longer than the existence of our species. ... But the use of this unprecedented power has had many worrisome consequences and has resulted in changes whose continuation might imperil the very foundations of modern civilization.'[9] And he is correct, except perhaps for the word 'might', which should more appropriately be replaced with the word 'will'. In the face of such existential threats, the discipline and professions of architecture and design (along with many other disciplines and many other professions) have turned their attention to issues of climate change and its related counterparts: ecology, sustainability, adaptation, resilience, etc. But the project of architecture is not enough. The project of 'insert-other-discipline-here' is not enough. Climate change is a problem so wicked, so scalarly complex, that an equally comprehensive unit is necessary – that of Civilisation. In the words of Rania Ghosn and El Hadi Jazairy, founders of the Boston-based research practice Design Earth, 'The environmental crisis can be seen not only as a crisis of the physical and technological environments; it is also a crisis of the cultural environment – of the modes of representation through which society relates to the complexity of environmental systems. ... the weather is experienced locally, while understanding the global effects of climate change would require perceiving the world as a whole.'[10]

It is this big-picture approach – and the inherent interdisciplinarity it necessitates – that makes work such as that of Design Earth so compelling. It continues and expands on the legacy of the unitary worldview of the late 18th- to early 19th-century German geographer, naturalist and explorer Alexander von Humboldt, who 'presented the earth in a range of scales from the micro to the macro, so that the eye took in the object as a whole then and proceeded to distinguish the parts until the totality was grasped as an assemblage of essential attributes'.[11] Similar to the project of Science before it split into many disciplines,[12] the project of Civilisation embeds a fail-safe against mono-disciplinary obsessions or solutions. And it is implicit that these 'solutions', if any, must hybridise and syncretise multiple perspectives, not be born from a singular one. Such a project is one of pluralism.[13]

And of course, climate change is not the only problem that benefits from a Civilisational lens. Even certain challenges at the scale of the city should more often be approached from an interdisciplinary angle. The Center for Civilization's Civic Commons Catalyst (CCC) initiative[14] began by looking at the question of underutilised spatial assets in Calgary, through six simultaneous disciplines/

research methods: urban design, public engagement (interviews), future studies (horizon scanning), public policy, finance innovation, and geospatial data and cartography. It has expanded to involve three additional municipalities, as well as project partners in industry, the community (such as non-profits), and various other academic units beyond the University of Calgary School of Architecture, Planning and Landscape (such as the School of Public Policy and the Haskayne School of Business). The CCC initiative does not break new ground in terms of individual methodologies or partnerships. Various multi-modal and complex projects in the field exist. The ambition is instead to approach an 'architectural' or 'urbanistic' question from various valuable 'external' perspectives. It needed to be approached from the lens of public policy, needed to cross-fertilise insights from finance innovation, needed to align with identified signals and trends from a horizon-scanning process. In scalar terms, the city was analysed at the level of the municipality, the province (Alberta) and the country (Canada). Not only was the physical built environment of the city put under the microscope, but so was its societal context mined for opportunities – a Civilisational approach.

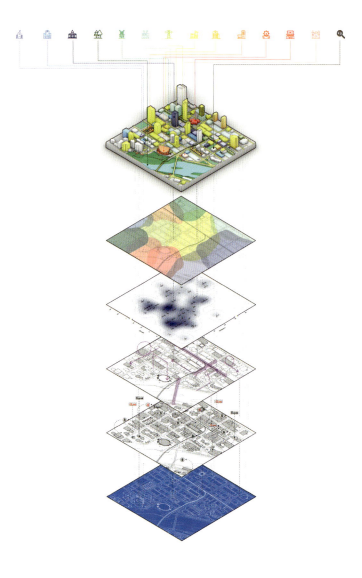

Alberto de Salvatierra and Anagha Patil /
Center for Civilization,
Civic Commons Catalyst (CCC):
Supporting Transformative Revitalisation
of Underutilised Spatial Assets
in Albertan Cities, Downtown Calgary,
Alberta, Canada, 2021

Exploded axonometric showing the six disciplinary /research elements of the CCC initiative.

Alberto de Salvatierra and Ji Song Sun/
Center for Civilization, Civic Commons
Catalyst (CCC): Supporting Transformative
Revitalisation of Underutilised Spatial
Assets in Albertan Cities, Downtown Calgary,
Alberta, Canada, 2021

Axonometric of the CCC catalogue of underutilised spatial assets in Calgary, which includes vacant buildings, vacant floors, vacant plots of land, car parks and public civic infrastructures.

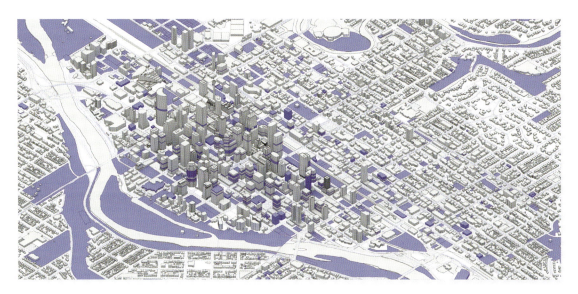

The Apocalypse of our Times

At the time of writing, Russia is invading Ukraine. But in contrast to the financial strategy of containment that the US-led NATO wants to effectuate in this conflict, a Civilisational lens will reveal the interconnectedness of the various players and why this war will escalate – most surely with dire consequences. The answer lies in material flows. In the most reduced and simplest of terms, as the economist Umair Haque explains: 'Russia keeps China's lights on – it is China's biggest supplier of electricity, one of its biggest suppliers of gas and coal and food and so forth. China pays for all that by selling [America/the West] cheap household goods … We are paying China, and China is paying Russia.'[15] This triangular trade demonstrates just how absurd trying to 'contain' Russia really is. Because no matter what, the West is still financing Putin's war machine via China. Zooming out further, these questions of material flows reveal the well-accepted fact that an over-reliance on fossil fuels has generated not only warfare, but climate crises that are likely to spur other regional or even global conflicts (water, anyone?). And all of these *wicked*, *sobering* problems (the pandemic, climate change, the war in Ukraine) are clearly headed towards a destructive crescendo – an 'apocalypse' of sorts. What will we find on the other side? Will the entrenched and skewed systems and hierarchies of power be reified and manifest some darker techno-enabled totalitarian dystopia? Or will the precariousness of these constructs finally come crashing down, giving way to new and more sustainable – and inclusive – modalities of society? The answer will be determined by our priorities, the peoples we bring to the table, and the identities, cultures and wisdoms we choose to include. To ensure our salvation, we must engage the whole of Civilisation. ᴆ

Notes

1. Aldous Huxley, *Island*, Chatto & Windus (London), 1962, p 132.
2. See Bruno Latour, 'The Abandonment of a Common World Leads to Epistemological Delirium', in *Down to Earth: Politics in the New Climatic Regime*, tr Catherine Porter, Polity Press (Cambridge), English edition, 2018, p 25.
3. Oxford Languages, Google's English dictionary: https://languages.oup.com/google-dictionary-en/.
4. See Kathryn Yusoff, *A Billion Black Anthropocenes or None*, University of Minnesota Press (Minneapolis, MN), 2018.
5. Bruno Latour, 'A Personal Defense of the Old Continent', in *Down to Earth*, op cit, p 102.
6. See TJ Demos, 'Anthropocene, Capitalocene, Chthulucene', in *Against the Anthropocene: Visual Culture and Environment Today*, Sternberg Press (Berlin), 2017, p 111.
7. See Alberto de Salvatierra, 'Eternal Ephemera: Soft Infrastructures in the Floating City of Uros, Peru', in Hannes Zander, Samantha Solano, Shelagh McCartney and Sonja Vangjeli (eds), *A Landscape Approach: From Local Communities to Territorial Systems*, AR+D Publishers (New York), 2022, pp 136–45.
8. *Ibid*.
9. Vaclav Smil, 'Fossil-Fueled Civilization', in *Energy and Civilization: A History*, MIT Press (Cambridge, MA), 2018, p 295.
10. Rania Ghosn and El Hadi Jazairy, 'Another Architecture for the Environment', in *Geostories: Another Architecture for the Environment*, Actar (Barcelona), 2018, p 11.
11. *Ibid*, p 19.
12. *Ibid*.
13. See Alberto de Salvatierra, Samantha Solano and Joshua Vermillion, 'Pedagogical Pluralism', in Samantha Krukowski (ed), *T-Squared: Theories and Tactics in Architecture and Design*, Intellect Books (London), 2022, pp 44–60.
14. See Center for Civilization, 'Civic Commons Catalyst: Supporting Transformative Revitalization of Underutilized Spatial Assets in Albertan Cities': https://centerforcivilization.org/projects/civic-commons-catalyst.
15. Umair Haque, 'Why We're Entering a New Era of War', *Eudaimonia and Co*, 1 March 2022: https://eand.co/is-the-world-going-back-to-war-a0a086c43f96.

Alberto de Salvatierra and Tripty Kaur / Center for Civilization, Climate + Catastrophe: Mapping Global Landscapes and Gradients of Crisis and Risk, 2022

Apocalypse map: world gradient. Geospatial visualisation that includes global gradients of risk across multiple categories (earthquakes, hurricanes, drought, sea-level rise, volcanic eruptions, oil spills, nuclear reactors), all colour-coded to a uniform gradient to highlight areas with more or less risk.

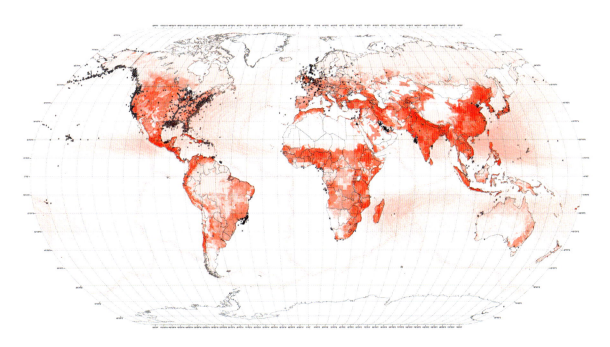

Text © 2022 John Wiley & Sons Ltd.
Images © Alberto de Salvatierra + the Center for Civilization

Lucía Jalón Oyarzun

Digital Doubles

The Major Agency of Minor Bits

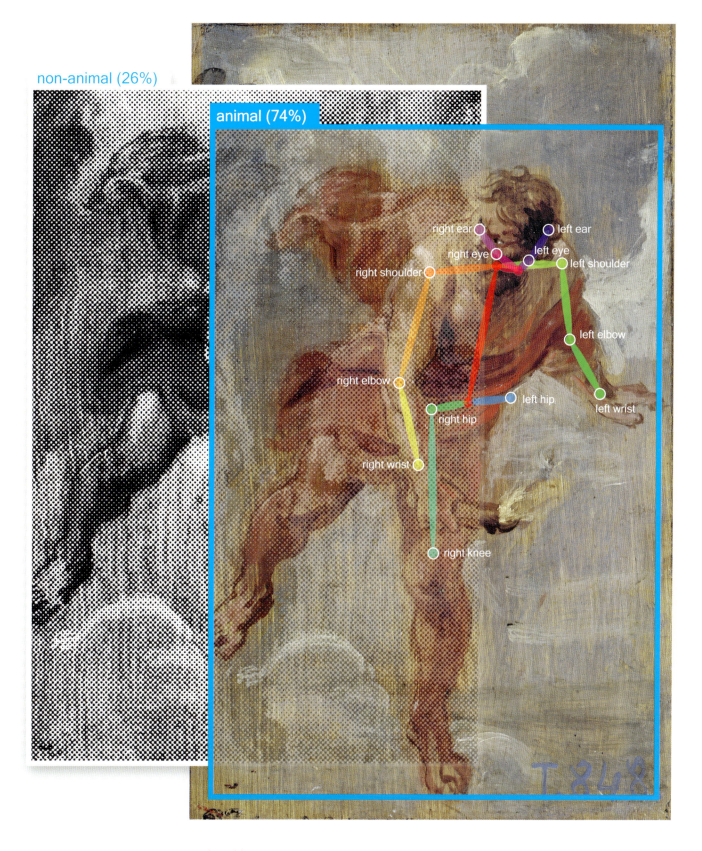

Lucía Jalón Oyarzun,
An alien practice in the
crevices of Promethean
instrumental reason,
2022

Google's Vision API defines Peter Paul Rubens' *Prometheus* (1636) as Animal (74%), leaving 26% of unaccounted vibrancy. Meanwhile, the OpenPose real-time multi-person human pose detection library for body, face, hands and foot estimation detects only 15 out of its standard 18 key points to define a human body.

In a world that seeks to describe, codify and quantify everything, and particularly our viscerality and its interactions with our actual and digital environments, can we find interstitial spaces, currently unseen, unobserved and unlegislated, where we might be able to create minor architectures capable of blooming? Architect and interdisciplinary researcher Lucía Jalón Oyarzun reveals where these spaces might be found.

Lucía Jalón Oyarzun,
A paradoxically accurate
43% of blurred uncertainty,
2022

Google's Vision API applied to Pieter Bruegel the Elder's *Tower of Babel* (*c* 1563) confirms that there is a building in the image with a 57% certainty.

Although we often confuse refusal with a passive exercise of rejection that stops within the limits of a no, its movement is always built upon the assertion of a horizon of possibility, a margin to do things otherwise, to breathe and take in the emergence of alternative worlds and futurities. In *Black Skin, White Masks* (1952), psychiatrist and essayist Frantz Fanon wrote that revolt does not yield on abstract reasoning; on the contrary, one revolts because it becomes 'impossible to breathe'.[1] The body revolts because it refuses the excision of the possible from its existence; the possible being an expression of the abundance of minor existences surrounding us, a fog of images, beginnings, potentialities, emergent qualities awaiting to be intensified, realised by an embodied and undisciplined architectural or world-making impulse: 'the possible, the possible, or I shall suffocate!'[2]

Lucía Jalón Oyarzun,
A disjointed assemblage of points,
2022

Leonardo da Vinci's *Vitruvian Man* (*c* 1490) processed with the OpenPose library to assign the 18 key points for pose detection.

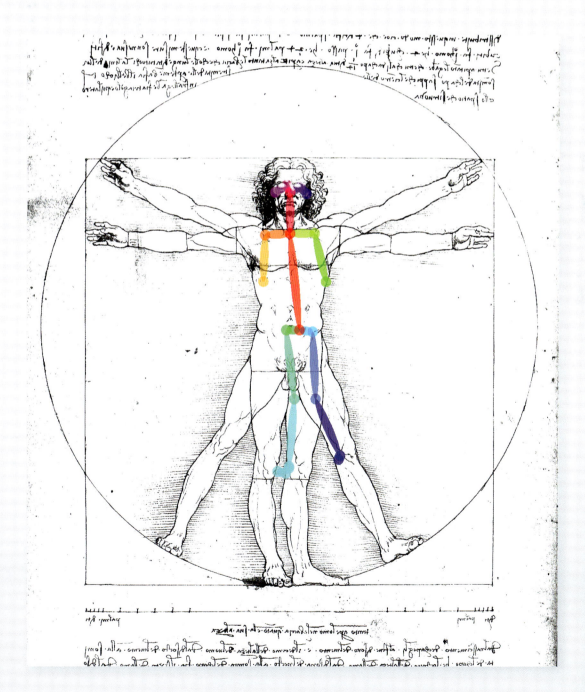

On 17 July 2014, Eric Garner was put in a chokehold while saying he could not breathe several times before expiring.[3] His desperate cry would soon become a key chant of the Black Lives Matter movement. Political thinker Franco Berardi would echo those words to acknowledge a growing physical and psychological breathlessness as a disconnect from that surrounding field of potentialities where only a world-making act – for Berardi poetry, for us here (minor) architecture – can thread our present with the possible to reactivate breathing and reopen the world to unscripted action.[4]

In the Southern black community where writer and activist bell hooks grew up, 'talking back' meant refusing the ban set upon a girl to speak freely and poetically to open a margin for breathing. This act of risk and daring was born upon the poetic language of black women at home, 'touching our world with their words'.[5] Talking back pushed the limits of the world, becoming a poetic world-making act: 'moving from silence into speech is for the oppressed, the colonized, the exploited, and those who stand and struggle side by side a gesture of defiance that heals, that makes new life and new growth possible.'[6]

It is this world-making power that expands refusal beyond rejection, and we must acknowledge the value and creativity enacted therein as well as consider its architectural dimensions. Architecture here is understood as the expression of an embodied agency to produce worlds, establish relations and thread the commons grounding a habitat. Refusal as assertion of a saturated possible amplifies the architectural agency of our bodies, both individual and collective, by taking in and making room for those minor existences to collaborate with their productive potential.

Remainders of Discretisation
The fog of minor existences surrounding us also expresses a material fuzziness, an entangled continuity of the world in which we discover ourselves necessarily inscribed. Nothing and no one can remain unaffected or untouched by the world. Material fuzziness asks from us an active disposition, for we must interpret the unfinished and imagine the yet unseen to realise possibilities. The world involves us through the noise it produces, inviting us to 'conspire' with it. Let us not forget that at the Latin root of this term, '*conspirare*', we find simply a breathing *with,* a breathing *together*.

Maths taught us as children how to call what does not fit in a division or a subtraction the 'remainder'. In his 2005 novel of the same name, writer Tom McCarthy tells the story of a man who suffers an accident involving 'technology, parts, bits' falling from the sky and must subsequently reconfigure his whole body and relearn how to do even the simplest gestures.[7] These movements are turned into discrete units so that walking or eating can be rewired into his body. However, this process has also induced a disquiet; there is some authenticity missing in his moves, a lively flow that made them genuine. It is that remainder that refuses discretisation

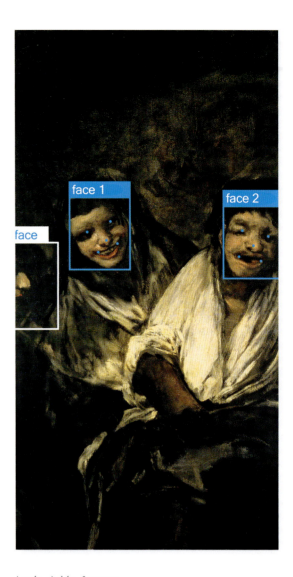

Lucía Jalón Oyarzun,
Disembodied patterns
overshadowing difference,
2022

The computer vision platform Amazon Rekognition pre-trained for facial attribute detection labels Francisco de Goya's *Women Laughing* (or *Man Mocked by Two Women*) (1820–23) as face 1, deemed to be a 6- to 14-year-old female (99.9%), not smiling (54.6%), and face 2 a female (50.6%), not smiling (89.4%) with the mouth closed (72.6%). The third face is incomputable.

and codification because it is impossible to fit into his now fully coded condition. Its constantly felt lack will make his short-circuited body fall into a doomed quest to capture and recode the lost continuity of his gestures.

Discretisation seeks to nullify remainders, eliminating the noise to transform the world's material fuzziness into a high-resolution image. It operates by short-circuiting affective continuities and classifying differences according to parameters that can be measured with precision, thus leaving all those minor existences, whose frail existence rejects identification and quantification, out of its attention. McCarthy's informated body shares some familiar roots with the vision of the body advanced by the cyberneticians as a disembodied pattern of information.[8] We see this clearly in the models training machines to detect and follow bodies, where flesh is discarded in favour of isolated key points locating ankles, knees and elbows, and where unnecessary skeletal lines linking them are an aesthetic concession to human vision. We find in this disjointed assemblage of points the only architectural body apparently able to surpass the influence of the Vitruvian Man and the premises of a modern regime of representation based on projective geometry and its corollary of subject and object. The body defining spatial production today is a flattened informational pattern, its breathing mere numbers of oxygen values on a smart-watch screen. Around it, architecture becomes data management, with drawn marks and traces substituted by electrical signals as the physical world is transformed into clouds of coloured points with no geometry, just information.[9]

Digital Doubles
Absolute discretisation liquifies the physical world, rephrasing every material entity as an addressable item, easily indexed and queried. The resulting coded environments are couplings of matter and digital doubles, informational doppelgängers producing a ghostly but efficient 'technology of the surrounds'.[10] The fog of minor existences is dispersed by clouds of discrete information, a distributed interface reshaping spatial agency on the fly.

The use of digital doubles, models reproducing with accuracy any given thing from cells to planets, has increased significantly in the last decade. Within architecture, it is almost old news to acknowledge the transformation brought by BIM by placing at the centre of design processes the digital smart modelling of buildings, from then on equated to countless discrete parts joined through interlinked databases. Unlike the architectural models of old that were transitory in-formational objects destined for the bin or the archive once they had fulfilled their role, these digital doubles accompany their physical counterparts far beyond completion (for example, of a building), orienting and shaping each other in real time while feeding on their continued interaction. They are meaningful agents of spatial production, though not because of an inessential built object; they are spatially efficient, in the aforementioned world-making sense,

Discretisation seeks to nullify remainders, eliminating the noise to transform the world's material fuzziness into a high-resolution image

Lucía Jalón Oyarzun,
A day will come when the magic
spell will be shaken off,
2022

Google's Vision API estimates that Mose Bianchi's *Woman in front of a Mirror* (*c* 1900) is a person with 66% probability. The percentage goes up to 75% when the fauna of the mirrors is added to the image file.

Lucía Jalón Oyarzun,
A distributed, more-than-human
creative potential,
2022

Google's Vision API considers only some of the moths and butterflies in Herman Strecker's collection of *Lepidoptera, rhopaloceres and heteroceres, indigenous and exotic; with descriptions and colored illustrations* (1872). The rest are left flying in an apparently incomputable limbo.

Major architecture's language is expanded to include proprietary algorithms, digital doubles and discrete data flows

through the interfacing environmentality produced in-between physical reality and its digital double. It is this real-time spatial production that is architecturally (and politically) meaningful, for it modulates practices, gestures and behaviours with extraordinary power and consequences. What was previously done through walls and enclosures operates here through the soft touches and nudges of a minutely designed milieu, articulated by the haptic qualities of pervasive and distributed computing.

In his *Book of Imaginary Beings* (1957), Argentine writer Jorge Luis Borges wrote a small fable on the 'Fauna of Mirrors', telling the story of a time when the 'world of mirrors and the world of men were not, as they are now, cut off from each other'.[11] They were quite different and lived in harmony, until one day the mirror people invaded the Earth, and after the war that ensued men used their 'magic' to imprison them in mirrors, 'and forced on them the task of repeating, as though in a kind of dream, all the actions of men'.[12] Remember here science-fiction writer Arthur C Clarke's words that 'any sufficiently advanced technology is indistinguishable from magic'.[13] Stripped from their power and their forms, the mirror people were reduced to slavish reflections. The short story finishes with a warning, for 'a day will come when the magic spell will be shaken off'.[14] We can picture that shaking off happening already, as our digital doubles start defining our spatial actions and world-making practices, nudging us to follow their beat.

Reframing the Major to Keep Tracing the Minor

However, we can also imagine their revolt as a refusal of the discretisation process they were subjected to, thus an assertion of the remainder still with them and its world-making potential. That slight vibration around their edges, a sign there is some breathing going on there, expresses the fuzziness of the possible, the abundance of minor existences and their architectural promises still awaiting the art capable of intensifying their reality.

Minor architectures can be thought of as belonging to that art, uncodifiable and undisciplined, an open repertoire of spatial practices and know-hows attentive to the differentiating agency of the real, feeding on the circumstantial and experimental.[15] The minor always exists in the narrow margins and blind spots of major languages, structures and knowledges, unsettling them, blurring their clear definitions and codifications. However, if major architecture has been traditionally defined by the old disciplinary posts of academia, journals and other authorial figures of architectural myth and stardom, today it has computation and its gendered, racist and capitalist roots at its core. Major architecture's language is expanded to include proprietary algorithms, digital doubles and discrete data flows, while the authorial figures are no longer architects but Autodesk, IBM or Alphabet.

'Our encryption is the real world.' Those are the words used by the leader of an anti-capitalist hacker cell in the 2015 US TV series *Mr Robot* to respond to the incredulity shown by his latest recruit, despondent cybersecurity engineer Elliot Alderson, bewildered to see they all work together in an old arcade at Coney Island instead of hiding behind encrypted digital identities. While IPs and codes render everything traceable, the noise, fuzziness and granularity of the 'real world' overcomes the discrete flatness of cyberspace. Discretisation and digital doubling generate a new regime of visibility, pre-empting, but not replacing, the fog of minor existences stirring the minor. When we submit Flemish artist Pieter Bruegel the Elder's *Tower of Babel* (*c* 1563) to Google's Vision AI application programming interface (API), it replies with a 57 per cent possibility that the canvas depicts a building, thus enclosing (to overshadow it) the remainder within an unmentioned statistic: a paradoxically accurate 43 per cent of blurred uncertainty. Minor existences, as the liveliness of the world's breathing, are incomputable. While rejecting discretisation, they reclaim a distributed, more-than-human creative potential: an alien practice emerging within the crevices of Promethean instrumental reason.

Refusal, conceived as the assertion of a horizon of possibilities and its architectural potentialities, intimately relates to this evolving and expanding major language. In its margins and blind spots, a minor repertoire of spatial practices keen on conspiring, noise, remainders and material fuzziness holds the potential to think and practise what architecture can be (and do) in the face of the challenges of our time. The possible, the possible or *we* will suffocate. ⌂

Notes

1. Frantz Fanon, *Black Skin, White Masks*, Pluto Press (London), 1986, p 226.
2. Gilles Deleuze, 'L'actuel et le virtuel', in *Dialogues*, Gallimard (Paris), 1996, pp 179–81; David Lapoujade, *Les existences moindres*, Éditions de Minuit (Paris), 2017. The final formula has often been attributed to Kierkegaard, for instance by Gilles Deleuze and Félix Guattari in *What Is Philosophy?*, Columbia University Press (New York), 1994, p 177.
3. Al Baker, J David Goodman and Benjamin Mueller, 'Beyond the Chokehold: The Path to Eric Garner's Death', *The New York Times*, 13 June 2015: www.nytimes.com/2015/06/14/nyregion/eric-garner-police-chokehold-staten-island.html.
4. Franco 'Bifo' Berardi, *Breathing: Chaos and Poetry*, Semiotext(e) (California), 2018, pp 10–15.
5. bell hooks, *Talking Back: Thinking Feminist, Thinking Black*, South End Press (Boston, MA), 1989, p 6.
6. Ibid, p 9.
7. Tom McCarthy, *Remainder*, Vintage Books (New York), 2005, p 3.
8. David Tomas, 'Feedback and Cybernetics: Reimaging the Body in the Age of the Cyborg', *Body & Society*, 1 (3–4), 1995, pp 21–43.
9. John May, *Signal. Image. Architecture*, Columbia University Press (New York), 2019, p 35; Dennis Häusler, Johannes Rebsamen and Matthias Vollmer, 'A Wall of Data Points', *Arch+, The Property Issue*, 2020, pp 174–83.
10. Beth Coleman, 'Right to the Smart City: How to Represent, Resist, or Disappear', in *Ways of Knowing Cities*, Columbia University Press (New York), 2019, p 147.
11. Jorge Luis Borges, *The Book of Imaginary Beings* [1957], Penguin Books (New York), 1974, p 67.
12. Ibid, p 68.
13. Arthur C Clarke, *Profiles of the Future: An Inquiry into the Limits of the Possible* [1962], Harper & Row (New York), 1974, p 21, n 1.
14. Borges, *op cit*, p 68.
15. Jill Stoner, *Toward a Minor Architecture*, MIT Press (Cambridge, MA), 2012. See also Lucía Jalón Oyarzun, *Exception and the Rebel Body: The Political as Generator of a Minor Architecture*, PhD thesis, Universidad Politécnica de Madrid, 2017: https://oa.upm.es/48250/.

Lucía Jalón Oyarzun, *Our encryption is the real world*, 2022

Jean François Millet's *Hunting Birds at Night* (1874) processed by Google's Vision API renders the two figures on the bottom, mixed with the fuzziness of nightly nature, as animals, while the standing figures above are labelled as 'person'. The OpenPose model also ignores the figures on the ground.

Text © 2022 John Wiley & Sons Ltd. Images © Lucía Jalón Oyarzun

Quilian Riano

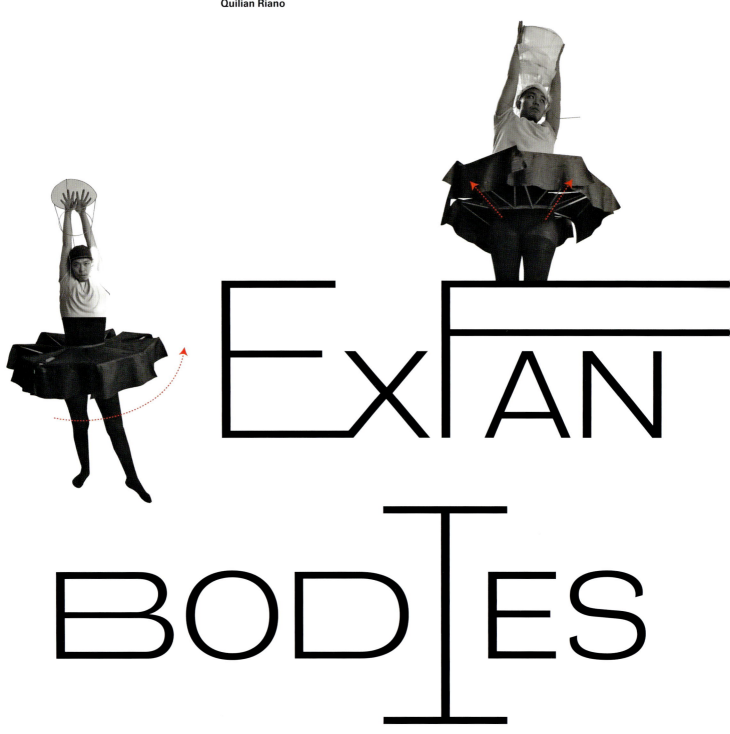

ExFan Bodies

PEDAGOGICAL MODELS FOR PLURALISTIC SPATIALITIES

Minette Murphy and
Thompson Cong Nguyen,
Body Exercise,
'Cooperative Futures' studio,
Carleton University,
Ottawa, Canada,
2021

For the Body Exercise, Murphy and Nguyen were inspired by professional dancer, artist and social worker Lexy Lattimore. During the 'Cooperative Futures' studio, Lattimore was leading art-based community engagement processes for a community urban plan of Hough, a majority African-American neighbourhood in Cleveland, Ohio. Murphy and Nguyen began to explore the tutu as a model for creating public space.

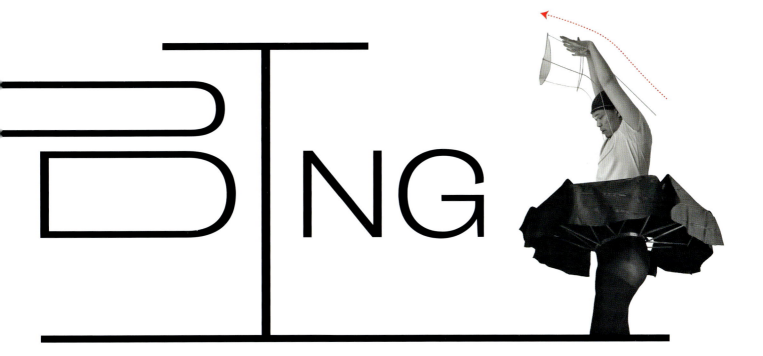

BUILDING

Depictions of ideal bodies, whether by Leonardo da Vinci or Le Corbusier, and their importation into the strictures of architecture and space-making generally, ignore a multitude of other bodies. **Quilian Riano**, Interim Dean of Pratt Institute's School of Architecture in Brooklyn, New York, looks at these other bodies and describes an inclusive, pluralistic future for architecture and the way it is taught.

The image is iconic. A man of whom we can see two different poses simultaneously, his arms are both spread to his side and lifted just a bit, his legs straight down and then just slightly opened. The pose is meant to create perfect shapes, with a square and circle superimposed around the body. Leonardo da Vinci's drawing, inspired by 1st-century-BC architect Vitruvius Pollio's writing, is meant to show the perfect human proportions and how it fits Platonic geometries. The drawing, however, brings up many questions. This body is very particular – male, seemingly Caucasian and able-bodied – leaving the viewer with the thoughts that for da Vinci (and Vitruvius) it may be the only kind of ideal body. No similar drawing exists showing other kinds of bodies, perhaps complicating and expanding the geometric impact on architectural space.

In 1943 architect Charles-Édouard Jeanneret, better known as Le Corbusier, introduced a new version when he began work on the Modulor Man – an anthropomorphic figure that seeks to create a single set of scales to design for. Yet, this figure stands at around 6 feet (1.8 metres) tall – 8 inches (20 centimetres) taller than the average height for a woman in the US.[1] Although clearly gendered, the Modulor Man, as drawn, lacks other characteristics, allowing it to stand for any body – a generic body shaping space.

As these bodies come into practice, they carry with them the assumptions made by their inventors. These bodies are male, they do not have any visible disabilities, they come from Europe. In this, they echo a larger issue that Western democracies are facing: implied subjectivity. The idea that given that institutions, such as governments and universities, were created by and for men of European descent, it is implied that they serve that demographic.

As the institutions become increasingly pluralistic, the question is whose bodies those institutions represent.

Yet centring bodies in architecture is important, and not only for scale and proportionality. By centring bodies and their everyday practices, new design and social potentials are unlocked. Instead of using generic bodies for the design of spaces, architectures, landscapes and urbanisms, centring bodies can reflect the uses of today and leave room for changes as bodies and groups change their practices.

Therefore, the problem left to architectural education and practice becomes one in which it has to re-imagine the very bodies it is designing for, as the abstraction of a universal human only serves to obscure what is really an implied subject.

Embodied Legacies in Design and Performance

In 1997 landscape architect Walter Hood published *Urban Diaries* as an attempt to use 'improvisation' in design. Part of the definition Hood gives to improvisation is that it reinforces the image of a community by using the familiar to validate 'the existence of multiple views of life in the city, even those that are outside the normative view.'[2] To do this, Hood employs diary entries as a way to understand the city of Oakland, California through its inhabitants, using these observations to create new spatial relationships and programmes. One example of the methodology can be found in the entry titled 'Day Four', where Hood writes about seeing a group of people heading to the park with alcoholic drinks in brown paper bags in their hands. He then explores the idea that this is no different from the beer gardens he has seen in Europe, saying: 'The beer garden is a simple programmatic

Minette Murphy and
Thompson Cong Nguyen,
Body Exercise,
'Cooperative Futures' studio,
Carleton University,
Ottawa, 2021, Canada,

Murphy and Nguyen continued to grow their work by considering a new actor: the children of Hough and how the tutu could grow to give them spaces for public performance.

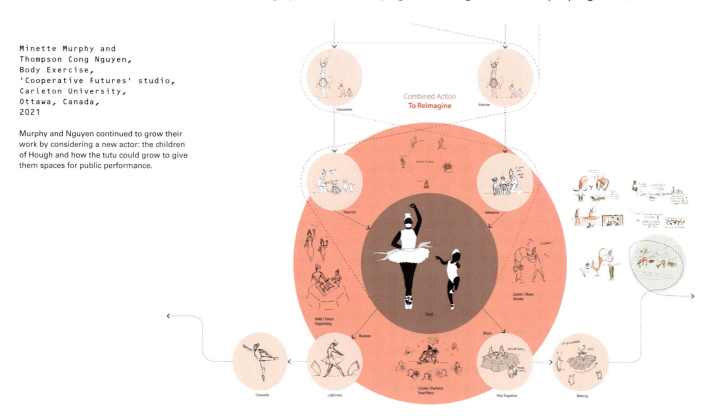

Walter Hood,
'Durant Minipark, Day Five: Recycling Bins',
diagram from *Urban Diaries*,
Oakland, California,
1997

Hood's diary of his observations of 1990s Oakland street life became diagrams and drawings of how individuals' everyday practices shape urban landscapes. These informed his designs for pluralistic new urban spaces intrinsically tied to their community, putting different users and uses into relationship. In this Day Five entry, Hood notes that the city government was denying individual collectors access to its recycling centres. To accommodate those users, he proposes recycling areas within a larger urban landscape that includes playgrounds, cultivation areas, etc.

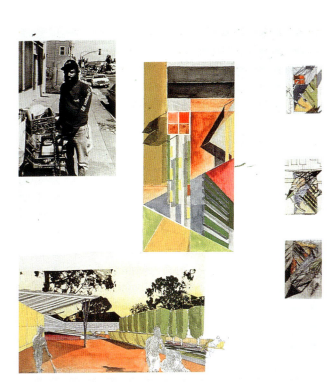

response to a familiar neighborhood use: it is not a place for beer sales, but a space to sit and relax, where beer consumption is accepted, not prohibited. With its trimmed rows of trees, seating, garden cultivation, and shelter at the street-side, the space is welcoming to the beer drinker. The familiar in this case is not judged but incorporated.'[3] Hood shows a methodology that uses careful study of individual bodies and communal everyday practices as a source of design.

Looking outside of architecture to find similar approaches, one can find Theatre of the Oppressed – a theatre style theorised in part by Brazilian theatre practitioner Augusto Boal that seeks potentially liberatory practices from the embodied experiences of individuals and groups facing oppression. Boal insists that the 'theatrical experience should begin not with something alien to the people (theatrical techniques that are taught or imposed) but with the bodies of those who agree to participate in the experiment.'[4] This process puts individuals at the centre of the performance and in turn in relationship with others potentially facing similar oppressions as a way to help see those individual and small group oppressions as part of a larger social and political system.

Both Hood's and Boal's work centres bodies and their everyday experiences to create new possibilities. Hood's work led to a series of new public space designs for Oakland, based on the stories collected throughout the fellowship period he documented. For Boal, centring bodies creates a window in the larger systems of power (political, economic and social), to image the processes that would allow the dismantling of moments of oppression.

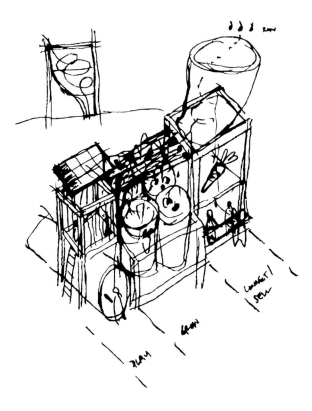

Minette Murphy and Thompson Cong Nguyen,
Bodies Negotiation,
'Cooperative Futures' studio,
Carleton University,
Ottawa, Canada,
2021

Concept sketch. After the Bodies Exercise, Murphy and Nguyen negotiated their work thus far with Mira Burghed and Rudo Mpisaunga whose group was doing work focused on the churches in Hough. This is a concept sketch from the early phase of this work.

Towards New Pedagogical Models

The Dark Matter University (DMU) is a BIPOC (black, indigenous and people of colour) collective of people involved in academia whose goal is to work within and outside of educational institutions to question and propose new antiracist pedagogical models. Founded in 2020, the DMU's first two studios took place at Carleton University in Ottawa, in winter 2021 and included 'FOR–WITH: An Individual Practice Towards Collective Expression' taught by Jelisa Blumberg and Curry Hacket and 'Cooperative Futures' taught by Jenn Low and myself – all core members of the DMU collective. 'Cooperative Futures' was also taught in collaboration with an Urban Design and Architecture studio that I led at Kent State University's College of Architecture and Environmental Design, Ohio.

The two studios at Carleton and the one at Kent were all sited in the community of Hough in Cleveland, Ohio, a majority African-American neighbourhood that is still reeling from its designation as a redlined community in the mid-1950s and the following decades of systematic public and private disinvestment. DMU seeks to create academic collaborations at all levels – from asking institutions to work with each other to co-teaching every course. Establishing large institutional and educational collaborations, such as the one created for the Hough-sited studios, allows the students to work with many community partners, design educators and even with students at other institutions.

From Body to Bod(ies)

'Cooperative Futures' postulated that the future in Hough really lies with the people already making change on the ground. Thus, a process was created by which the students heard from and focused on the individuals working in Hough, for example creating technology cooperatives, new parks and writing fellowships. A complicating factor, however, was how to create a truly collaborative process for the studios, given the remote modality forced by the Covid-19 pandemic.

A studio process was thus created that gamified collaboration. The students began by designing furniture-sized pieces to fit the bodies of individuals they had talked to and/or researched within the community. From then, the students were asked to negotiate with one other group – to look at the furniture-scaled piece they had designed for their individual and to find places of commonality or difference. After the conversations and negotiations, both groups were asked to consider how to mutate their design given the one they had just seen and scale up to design something that would accommodate a larger group of people (potentially including their original individual as well as the one the group they negotiated with designed for).

Each group then kept scaling up from one body, to a few bodies, all the way to the urban design scale. At the end of the semester, each project was grounded on the community, held the DNA of the other projects and

right: At the end of the semester, Murphy and Nguyen created The Pink Tutu, a toolkit of spatial strategies and processes that would allow the community in Hough to quickly test out new spatial configurations in areas of their choosing. The strategies could be used in large urban areas, such as the ones surrounding the cultural hub around the urban vineyard Chateau Hough.

Minette Murphy and
Thompson Cong Nguyen,
The Pink Tutu,
'Cooperative Futures' studio,
Carleton University,
Ottawa, Canada,
2021

above: The spatial strategies of The Pink Tutu can also be used in smaller-scaled spaces such as the porches that are currently important public spaces in Hough.

Incubator Space
Collective Mapping Workshops

Potential Collaborators

Youth Council   Artist / Community Builder   Children / Emerging Artist

Weekend Performances - Advocacy and Arts

Alice Won and Yakine Zerrad,
Live, Work and Play
Cooperative Building,
'Cooperative Futures' studio,
Carleton University,
Ottawa, Canada,
2021

right: At the end of the semester, Won and Zerrad created a series of live-work spaces for the artists living and coming to Hough. They used these new housing arrangements to also create play spaces for the community's children. All these were thought of as a community land trust, potentially run by existing arts groups.

Alice Won and Yakine Zerrad,
Actors and Shared Typologies
diagram,
'Cooperative Futures' studio,
Carleton University,
Ottawa, Canada,
2021

below: Won and Zerrad focused on Twelve Literary Arts, a group that holds a fellowship that brings artists and writers to the community. In 2021, Twelve Literary Arts was also leading a process by which young people in Hough used writing as a way to re-imagine their urban spaces. Won and Zerrad also worked closely to identify the needs of many actors, creating a catalogue of spatial typologies that could be recombined to fulfil current and future needs.

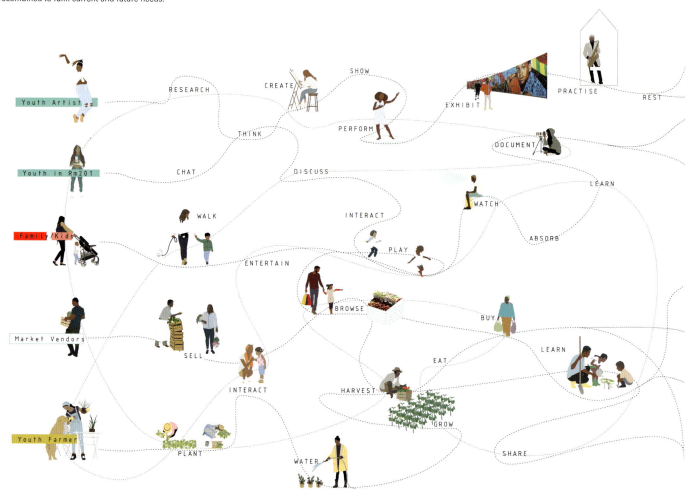

took into consideration multiple individuals and groups – mothers, urban farmers, students in the local schools, performers, and the writer fellowship that already existed.

One of the partners in the studio was Cleveland Owns, a community-based network of cooperatively owned ventures that provide services like internet and solar energy. Given this interest within, each project was further required to think about how it could be run by a community-based cooperative so that economic, social and spatial change could reinforce each other. For example, a Carleton group made up of Mira Burghed and Rudo Mpisaunga studied the history and role of churches in Hough. The study of local conditions was paired with research into both the black commons[5] and how the black church in the US has created cooperatives and community-based building processes that have developed, for example, housing as well as public and market spaces. Their project proposed a new kind of cooperative led by churches in Hough that would begin by transforming the public spaces and move on to creating housing and other urban amenities.

Pluralistic Futures

Generally, the generic body in space has been seen as a benign, necessary conceit. It helps bring the body scale right into the design of objects, architectures and cities. Yet these bodies have never truly been generic, as such a body does not exist. Rather, these are abled bodies, gendered bodies, racialised bodies, that create implied norms for others to follow. This is an issue that extends beyond space, with many of our institutions holding 'implied subjectivities' of the bodies that the institution is meant to serve.

Groups like the Dark Matter University were created to challenge the implied subjectivity of architectural education and to re-imagine the bodies and subjectivities it serves. Furthermore, to re-imagine the pedagogical place as a place to envision pluralistic pedagogies and processes that may lead to spaces where that pluralism can play out.

The 'Cooperative Futures' studios were an attempt to create such new pedagogical models – centring bod(ies) through collaborative design processes. No longer centring the 'generic' or 'universal' bodies that prioritise specific gender, racial and ethnic traits even when not intended, but centring real bodies and their everyday practices. These bodies, to reach pluralism, then need to be put in negotiation and conversation with other real bodies and the systems they represent, mutating each other's needs and creating collective growth. Instead of perfect proportions, they seek to instigate the kinds of perfect negotiations that create pluralistic spaces. ⌂

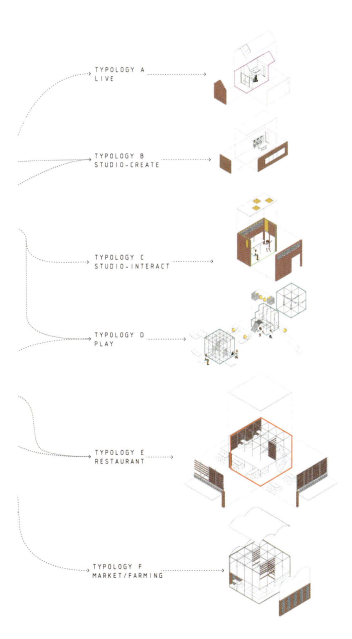

Notes
1. US Centers for Disease Control and Prevention (Cheryl D Fryar, Deanna Kruszon-Moran, Qiuping Gu and Cynthia L Ogden), 'Mean Body Weight, Height, Waist Circumference, and Body Mass Index Among Adults: United States, 1999–2000 Through 2015–2016', *National Health Statistics Reports* 122, 20 December 2018, p 6.
2. Walter Hood, *Urban Diaries*, Spacemaker Press (Washington DC), 1997, p 6.
3. *Ibid*, p 18.
4. Augusto Boal, *Theater of the Oppressed*, tr Charles A and Maria-Odilia Leal McBride, Pluto Press (London), 2008, p 103 (originally published in 1974 as *Teatro del Oprimido*).
5. Julian Agyeman and Kofi Boone, 'Could Collective Ownership of a "Black Commons" Help Advance Economic Justice?', *Fast Company*, 19 June 2019: www.fastcompany.com/90518679/could-collective-ownership-of-a-black-commons-help-advance-economic-justice.

Text © 2022 John Wiley & Sons Ltd. Images: pp 38–40, 41(b), 42–3 © Minette Murphy and Thompson Cong Nguyen; p 41(t) © Walter Hood; pp 44–5 © Alice Won and Yakine Zerrad

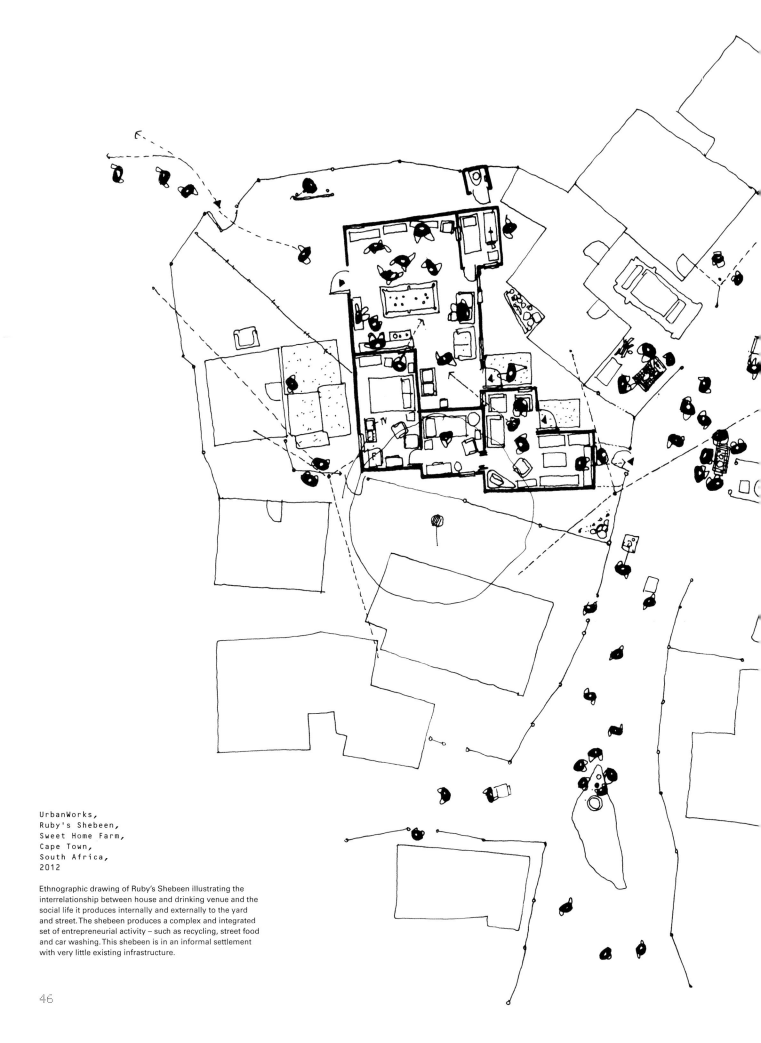

UrbanWorks,
Ruby's Shebeen,
Sweet Home Farm,
Cape Town,
South Africa,
2012

Ethnographic drawing of Ruby's Shebeen illustrating the interrelationship between house and drinking venue and the social life it produces internally and externally to the yard and street. The shebeen produces a complex and integrated set of entrepreneurial activity – such as recycling, street food and car washing. This shebeen is in an informal settlement with very little existing infrastructure.

Shebeen Operations
Navigating Deviance

Thireshen Govender founded Johannesburg-based design-research studio UrbanWorks as a means to read, speculate and intervene in urban situations. Here he illustrates how to look and decipher in a manner that provides tangible evidence for radical and realisable architectures in order to shift the trajectory of urban life in volatile contexts by deploying space and architecture as a political instrument.

The heart of history, for Heidegger, is not a sequence of occurrences but the eruption of significance at critical junctures that bring us into our own by making all being, including our being, into an urgent issue. In emergency, being emerges.
— Richard Polt writing on Martin Heidegger's philosophy, 2006[1]

The lived experience for the majority of those dwelling in South African cities is dire and volatile, due to an increasingly incapable state, limited resources and regressive political and social policies. A hopeful urban future seems out of reach. Refusal is a rejection of perpetuating exclusivity, inequality and bureaucracy in and through the existing systems of power. Through a careful discernment of the nature of refusal and its intelligently and reciprocally calibrated set of responses, however, UrbanWorks believes something radically speculative can emerge. This is refusal that can be deeply meaningful for architectures that operate in states of extreme volatility and trauma.

Antifragile Looking
The writer and statistician Nassim Nicholas Taleb's concept of the 'antifragile'[2] is especially valuable in guiding the framing and enquiry into the architecture of refusal. The antifragile encompasses things that gain in strength and function from exposure to stress and volatility. Architecturally, this provides an invaluable and conceptual lens to observe and discern what to look out for in order to locate these architectures within larger dynamic socio-political contexts. These architectures operate within sites of regressive social and political control. They are insurgent in nature – directly and subversively responding to power. Their attendant and resulting programmatic and spatial composition is cunningly complex. Being both insurgent and antifragile is how to discern an architectural refusal.

All parts of the city are implicated in the antifragile and insurgent architectural gaze. Some are more valuable than others – especially conditions in extreme flux that present some form of trauma and crisis. The attributes of these architectures are rather specific. They operate with a high degree of urgency, towards a crisis or opportunity. Their architectural materiality, power relations and functions correspond to this urgency – often rapidly configured and highly adaptable. These architectures also expand our imagination in how they are conceptualised and function due to their emergent attributes. Through their manifestation they forcefully and acutely create new opportunities for participation – especially for marginalised constituents who are less represented by the prevailing power politics. Most significantly, these architectures are transformative. They shift the existing centres of power, creating new subversive political and economic ecosystems that are place-specific. All of these are consistently undertaken with very limited resources and high degrees of appropriation.

The careful observation and documentation of insurgent architectures necessitates a temporary suspension of one's own subjectivity. It warrants an objective and critical look at what is legal and what is not – to avoid overlooking what is productive and inventive. The observation is acutely architectural, in the sense that it seeks out how an architecture produces a set of socio-political outcomes and is simultaneously produced by them. Sites are observed at multiple scales and through multiple objects and relations – seeking out the antifragile and insurgent is not passive documentation but coupled with the intent to redeploy these learnings to better effect. In deciphering productive socio-spatial relations and their constituent parts, the ability to 'recreate' and simulate these better effects forms an architecture of refusal.

The architectural practices and outcomes that are born out of extreme urban volatility and uncertainty can be antifragile. Carefully calibrated and iterative, these responses cumulatively produce a highly inventive and customised architectural response. The nature of the context constitutes a form of political violence – whereby the actors in these sites are rightfully or wrongfully denied meaningful participation. Restrictive policies on land uses, architectural configuration, function and participation (particularly of foreigners) result in responses that are clandestine and not endorsed by centres of power. As a result, these spatial responses and practices are subversive but also insurgent and create new centres of power through inventive means – challenging the legal frameworks that exist. The insurgent attribute produces a highly inventive architecture that also suggests more imaginative and inclusive ways of curating our cities.

The township is an urban settlement, located at the margins of economic centres, where black inhabitants were forced to live during South Africa's racialised apartheid regime. Highly regulated, properties were constrained to residential uses, limiting social and economic opportunities. This has created enormous tension in realising real economic opportunity for inhabitants, as recent policy changes have not altered apartheid uses – indeed, they have inadvertently reinforced them. Today, these townships are forcefully rejecting this through a collective and radical reimagination of homes, streets, mobility and trade. At this intersection of volatility and opportunity, new insurgent architectural typologies emerge, reconciling what is legal and what is not (yet).

Shebeen Dynamics: Toxicity and Deviance
Drinking, as practice, and specifically in townships, is entangled with a dark and repressive history of control of the urban black populace, through prohibition laws and the introduction of beer halls within townships by the apartheid state. It is paradoxically the sites of drinking, again, that are showing powerful socio-economic and political gravity in shaping the township. While the consumption of alcohol can occupy two extremes – one of toxic overindulgence and another of more social and recreational value – the latter is the focus here. Practised as a function of leisure, in an insurgent manner, it has profound transformative capacity in historical sites designed for extractive labour and retreat.

Most sites for drinking today are within adjusted homes called 'shebeens'. These shebeens create critical economic opportunity and provide a social amenity that is not adequately catered for by state authorities. Shebeens, functionally and spatially, are beyond the existing threshold of what is deemed legal – making the sites and their agents at risk of persecution. Consequently, the shebeen operates with variable thresholds of visibility (to its patrons) and concealment (from the authorities). This manoeuvring is done through the spatial composition and programming of spaces. The shebeen is often nested deep within settlements and private spaces with very conditional and layered access points.

To understand the nuances of how these insurgent architectures produce a more inventive urbanity, two South African shebeens – Ruby's Shebeen in Sweet Home Farm, Cape Town and Jack's Shebeen in Ivory Park, Johannesburg – are explored here. These granular explorations illustrate the sophisticated and radical transformation of the home into powerful social and economic infrastructures in marginalised and impoverished settings. The study of Eveline Street in Katutura, Windhoek, Namibia shifts the scale register to illustrate how these micro-architectures, with an enabling framework, are capable of making radically new urban spaces in resources-scarce contexts.

```
UrbanWorks,
Ruby's Shebeen,
Sweet Home Farm,
Cape Town, South Africa,
2012
```

below top: The shebeen interior is an enclosed social space that is an extension of the house which is thoughtfully mediated through objects, choice of patronage and nature of service. The carefully placed serving hatch allows the owner to engage and regulate the occupants via her kitchen.

below middle: The domestic and leisure functions are carefully managed by the shebeen owner who has a direct and active relationship to how the space is used by occupants. The internal window is a device through which the operator can be undertaking primary domestic activities whilst still controlling the shebeen through music and verbal instructions.

below bottom: Despite its discreet setting and modest interior operations, the shebeen generates significant social and economic life externally. This affects the neighbouring structures and street which plays host to complementary businesses such as recycling and street food.

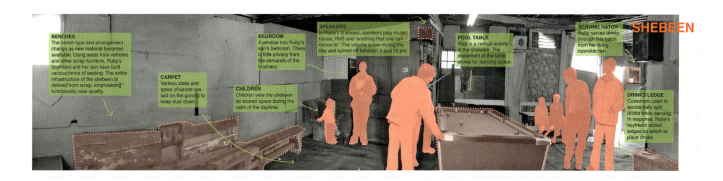

Through a study of these shebeens in an informal settlement (slum) – employing interviews, ethnographic drawings and photographs – the operations of these complex typologies have been documented. The work revealed the mechanics of how shebeens operate to mitigate risk and provide opportunity and how they are socially and materially produced to enable rich and complex socio-economic transactions. Homes have been ingeniously adapted to provide a powerful social asset within the neighbourhood: a space to socialise, meet, seek counsel and financial support. Often things denied by the state and its repressive policies, shebeens take on a profound and local institutional gravity. Their spaces are highly customised to respond to the changing living conditions of the home. Rooms are added or removed when children leave home or family members return to the city seeking refuge and opportunity. Their usually salvaged materials of corrugated iron, timber posts, doors, windows and simple assemblies allow for high levels of adaptability that is within the technical and physical capacity of their users. This allows for changes within the structure to be carried out immediately with little negotiation or friction – perpetually adapting between tensions of threat and opportunity.

These architectures are not static and empty – they are occupied and operated by a significant protagonist. Shebeen operators are powerful agents who inform the formal infrastructure and social composition of the shebeen. They manage the nature of patronage and atmosphere of the shebeen through the careful curation of type of alcohol, type of music, food offerings and furniture. The adjustment of these resources allows the operator to control the opening, closing, and volume of the crowd. These granular micro-adjustments work at the scale of the body, object and interior. The nature of change being small, responsive and cumulative, the process establishes a highly resilient – antifragile – typology. Collectively this creates a finely tuned and highly responsive typology that can move between the highly deviant and the highly productive, depending on the social and technical composition of the shebeen. The notion that this typology can be harnessed through design to have desirable and controlled outcomes is invaluable.

Shebeen Deployments: Building and Street

The transformational possibilities of the shebeen can exist at multiple scales, and when thoughtfully deployed, can have profoundly transformative effects. Leveraging the social and inclusive charge of the shebeen as a local moment can have meaningful agency in the larger public and urban realms.

Ruby's Shebeen illustrates a spatial configuration in the context of a slum condition with little-to-no infrastructure. The form is unregulated and dynamic. Jack's Shebeen illustrates how the shebeen can be integrated into more formal homes and bring highly complex and responsive sets of adaptations. The original house is indecipherable from the current configuration. The property has a street-facing tavern towards the neighbourhood road, a large wholesaler on the high street (previously the back of house), a distribution centre, additional residential units and a public alleyway to allow the public to pass through the private property. The shebeen demonstrates a powerful capacity to adapt to existing physical infrastructure and to refuse repressive and regressive policies, politics and top-down spatial logics.

The capacity of the shebeen and its set of micro-adjustments to shape a city is demonstrated in a study of a Namibian township high-street in Katutura, Windhoek. Leading up to 2008 the state authority took a bold and radical decision to decriminalise any business that traded within designated streets – with the intention of stimulating high streets in residential townships. The policy seemingly backfired when a proliferation of shebeens dominated the business profile within the early years of this policy adjustment. Over time (by 2016) this concentration of shebeens inadvertently brought increased business activity and diverse economic investment to the street, as well as high levels of economic inclusion – leveraging very limited resources with extremely high impact.

Over time Jack has incrementally added a series of extensions to his property – not all compliant, but highly functional. The tension between what is permissible versus what is enabling is brought into question as his investments have brought about an increased opportunity for his participants and the neighbourhood.

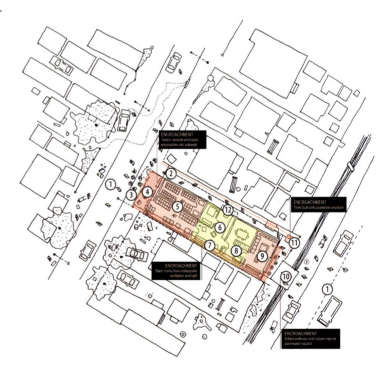

01. Neighbourhood street pavement
02. Driveway entrance
03. Pavement for pedestrian movement
04. Covered seating area (tavern)
05. Alcoholic drinks storage area
06. Kitchen
07. Rental rooms
08. Family rooms (above lounge and bedroom)
09. Spaza shop
10. Added walkway bridge over culvert
11. Toilet addition
12. Pedestrian throughway

Jack's Shebeen is different in the sense that it is located within existing infrastructure that it has adapted and appropriated. It has created both a front and back street condition, a side semi-public alleyway and a series of additions to the existing property.

UrbanWorks,
Jack's Shebeen,
Ivory Park,
Johannesburg,
South Africa,
2012

MATERIALS
01. Main house (brick)
02. Out toilet (brick)
03. Tavern storage area (brick)
04. Spaza shop (brick)
05. Additional toilet (brick)
06. Tavern seating area (steel)

PROGRAMME
01. Quiet neighbourhood street
02. Busy street
03. Pavement used for walking and drinking
04. Walkway placed over large stormwater culvert
05. Veranda for tavern seating
06. Tavern drinks storage
07. Main house (ground floor)
08. Spaza shop
09. Toilet
10. Toilet
11. Raised platform in front of spaza shop
12. Driveway and pedestrian thoroughfare
13. Main house (first floor)

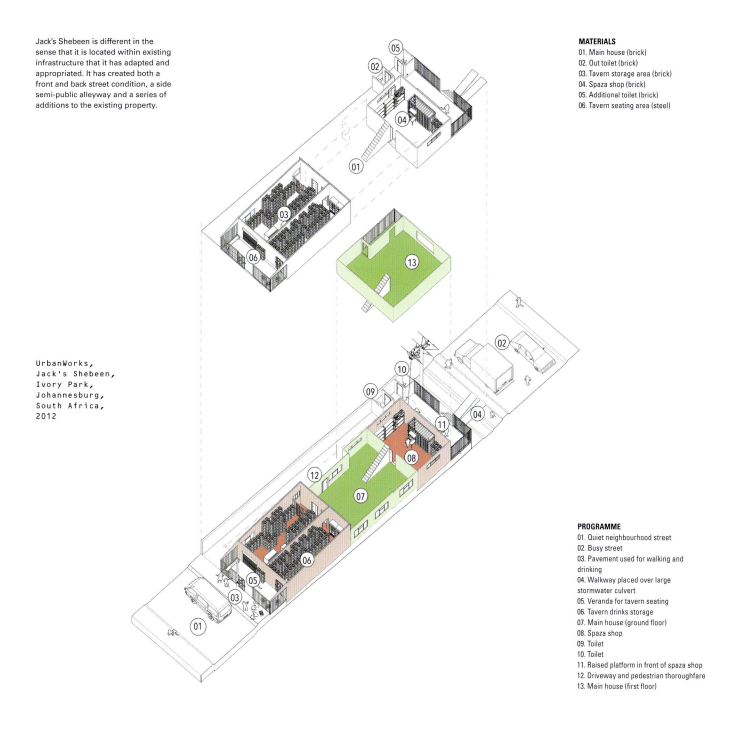

PUBLIC ROAD   PAVEMENT   PRIVATE PROPERTY   PAVEMENT   PUBLIC ROAD

UrbanWorks,
Eveline Street Shebeen,
Katutura,
Windhoek, Namibia,
2016

right: The inherited infrastructure of roads, plot and house, while not deliberately designed to allow adjustment, has been radically reimagined through the catalytic role of the shebeen and the enabling policy environment to legitimise trading on the high street. All available land has been carefully put to use.

below: The shebeens are directly contributing to the composition of the high street and constitute an interdependent ecosystem of related businesses such as car washes, hair salon, street food and mechanics. The original houses playing host to these ecosystems provide basic infrastructure such as water, storage and electricity while retreating to the background.

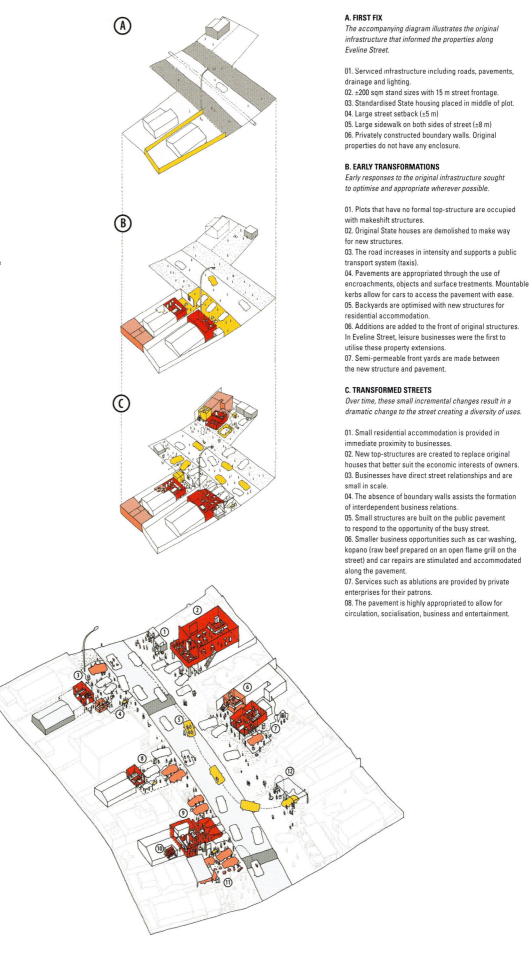

A. FIRST FIX
The accompanying diagram illustrates the original infrastructure that informed the properties along Eveline Street.

01. Serviced infrastructure including roads, pavements, drainage and lighting.
02. ±200 sqm stand sizes with 15 m street frontage.
03. Standardised State housing placed in middle of plot.
04. Large street setback (±5 m)
05. Large sidewalk on both sides of street (±8 m)
06. Privately constructed boundary walls. Original properties do not have any enclosure.

B. EARLY TRANSFORMATIONS
Early responses to the original infrastructure sought to optimise and appropriate wherever possible.

01. Plots that have no formal top-structure are occupied with makeshift structures.
02. Original State houses are demolished to make way for new structures.
03. The road increases in intensity and supports a public transport system (taxis).
04. Pavements are appropriated through the use of encroachments, objects and surface treatments. Mountable kerbs allow for cars to access the pavement with ease.
05. Backyards are optimised with new structures for residential accommodation.
06. Additions are added to the front of original structures. In Eveline Street, leisure businesses were the first to utilise these property extensions.
07. Semi-permeable front yards are made between the new structure and pavement.

C. TRANSFORMED STREETS
Over time, these small incremental changes result in a dramatic change to the street creating a diversity of uses.

01. Small residential accommodation is provided in immediate proximity to businesses.
02. New top-structures are created to replace original houses that better suit the economic interests of owners.
03. Businesses have direct street relationships and are small in scale.
04. The absence of boundary walls assists the formation of interdependent business relations.
05. Small structures are built on the public pavement to respond to the opportunity of the busy street.
06. Smaller business opportunities such as car washing, kopano (raw beef prepared on an open flame grill on the street) and car repairs are stimulated and accommodated along the pavement.
07. Services such as ablutions are provided by private enterprises for their patrons.
08. The pavement is highly appropriated to allow for circulation, socialisation, business and entertainment.

01. Micro-architectural encroachments
02. Large shebeen above existing house
03. Independent additions in private yard
04. Independent business cluster of food, car washing, repairs and hair care
05. Public taxis
06. Hair salon and shebeen cluster
07. Borrowed resources for car wash
08. Private street-facing yard
09. Street-facing bars with overhangs
10. Storage in existing house
11. Street food kiosk
12. Car wash

The shebeen demonstrates a unique capacity to operate within the crevices of urban conditions, transforming spaces rapidly through its transscalar application, and to shift its own profile from deviant to productive

Sheebeen Futures

In South Africa, the criminalisation of the shebeen for non-compliant uses and infringement relegates the typology to operate in the shadows of urban life. In Katutura, however, the micro-adjustments of residential properties catalysed by the proliferation of shebeens had an inverse effect – the shebeen jostled to be part of the street commons. In so doing it offered more inclusive social functions for a broader user group, including youth and women. It also brought with it other related businesses such as car washers, car mechanics, street food vendors, restaurants and hair salons. Each business unit held autonomous agency to respond to the opportunities of the street, based on available resources and social capital. The incremental and interdependent investments are not indiscriminately arranged, but carefully integrated into an enabling infrastructure. This infrastructure is both accidental and soft (policy). While accidental, these socio-economic ecosystems produced a vibrant street while harnessing the transformative value of the shebeen within eight years (2008–16), as seen in Katutura. The shebeen demonstrates a unique capacity to operate within the crevices of urban conditions, transforming spaces rapidly through its trans-scalar application – within the room, the house, the yard, the street and the neighbourhood – and to shift its own profile from deviant to productive.

A careful discernment of the architectural, social and infrastructural possibilities of the shebeen illustrates the transformative – antifragile and insurgent – capacity of architectures of refusal in volatile contexts. The first formal expressions of these typologies do not present themselves in clean, neat or even 'legitimate' guises; however, it is possible for the architect to draw out these productive and transformative mechanics in a manner that can be repurposed, re-curated and leveraged with a more inclusive agency. These indeterminate architectures do require a meta infrastructure through which to self-organise to have impact at the scale of the city. With a carefully curated and supportive infrastructure that harnesses the latent transformative capacity of rogue architectural typologies like the shebeen, necessary new urban imaginaries can be conjured – through granular acts of architecture. ᴆ

Notes
1. Richard Polt, *The Emergency of Being: On Heidegger's 'Contributions to Philosophy*, Cornell University Press (Ithaca, NY), 2006, p 5.
2. Nassim Nicholas Taleb, *Antifragile: Things That Gain from Disorder*, Random House (New York), 2012.

The shebeens are primary generators of urban form and activity and stand in sharp contrast to normative catalytic infrastructure provided by the state, such as bus stations and markets. There is a reciprocal relationship between the sedan taxis and the shebeens that enable rampant urban transformations.

Text © 2022 John Wiley & Sons Ltd.
Images © Thireshen Govender

Hannah le Roux

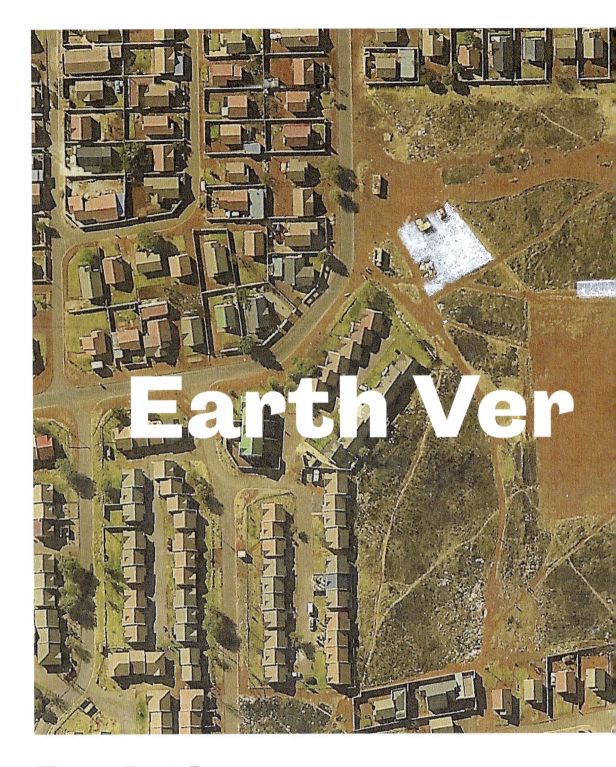

Earth Ver

Resisting Globalisation on the Open Pitch

sus FIFA

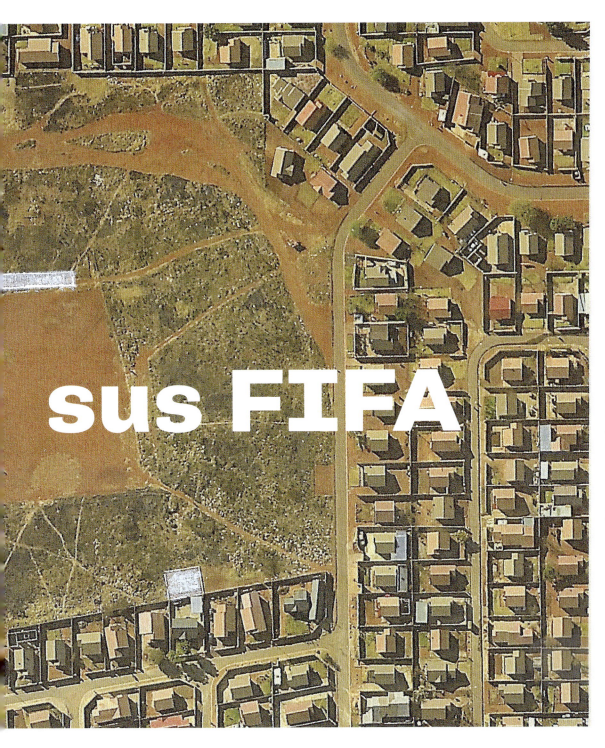

Hannah le Roux, Tent location on a township football field, 2022

The introduction of the 36-metre-long tents – shown here in crayon on an aerial photograph from a 2008 survey – creates a small-scale urban element in or along open fields, which could signal their capacity for more formal support structures.

Hannah le Roux is an architect and architectural historian specialising in the modern architecture of Southern Africa. An Associate Professor at the University of the Witwatersrand, here she documents the importance of football to local communities and its binding effect in strengthening societal bonds and providing a sense of self-determination.

There are football pitches all over South Africa, a legacy of the game's role as a site of embodied resistance in black communities. One can find them scraped out in open spaces: where there is housing, there are spaces to play football. On these pitches, reference to the Modernist model of a football field is ephemeral: at most, ash lines on the ground, and sometimes simply four temporary markers as goals. Such open pitches give a datum for alteration that is both robust – defended through use – and fragile – physically open. Where football fields were laid out by the government, whether during apartheid or more recently, their space has a very different quality, by virtue of their surfaces – usually grass – their fenced boundaries and their mono-functional use.

World Cup Legacies
These social and spatial contrasts were heightened by events running up to the 2010 FIFA World Cup, which promised to reduce these contrasts. But while South Africa's World Cup planning was presented in the 2003 Bid Book as a popular project and planned out as an event management exercise, the implementation largely benefited established construction companies.[1] The Bid Book's many images of children playing on dusty fields alongside informal settlements gave way to a representation of mega-projects and metrics. The official events took place without exception outside of townships – black residential areas. The 'legacy projects', funded with a fraction of the World Cup profits and planned as an ameliorative strategy for township football, were delayed and only a fifth of them were built.[2] In Alexandra, one of the densest townships near Johannesburg, a Football for Hope Centre was promised as the site for the Street Football event that ran during the World Cup, but nothing had been constructed by June 2010 and the event was housed in temporary structures.

The township projects that were built were mostly standardised, 'top-down' and even destructive interventions. In the region of Ekurhuleni to the east of Johannesburg, 24 out of a promised 64 'Legacy Fields' were identified, irrigated, planted with grass, surrounded with concrete palisade fences and locked. Most of these fields, which were previously managed within communities for leisure leagues, were later vandalised. Moreover, the South African Football Association (SAFA) chose to certify games played on turf only, leaving many townships without a field that could provide entry into leagues. Instead, SAFA only monitored a few formal sites, some renovated with artificial turf, benefiting those industries while draining local talent.[3]

The World Cup's recognition of football as South Africa's most popular sport and the presence of public attention also spurred the growth of non-governmental organisations around the game. But black self-organisation around football really did not require the state's or FIFA's interventions. The creation and management of teams and leagues was already a widespread activity that had grown alongside black urbanisation from the early 20th century. It was a medium through which individuals gained political, social and material success denied to them in formal, white-controlled organisations.[4] Access to grounds already happened through the borrowed use of pitches belonging to schools and colleges, mines, or through industry donations to the township administration boards.

Overgrown football field in KwaThema, South Africa, 2009

Open football fields allow overlapping uses. Their proximity to housing means residents often use them as shortcuts. In KwaThema, livestock graze on some fields. Their maintenance by the state is erratic.

Pipe goalposts at a football field in KwaThema, 2009

As a social commons, rather than a place owned by an institution, the open fields rely on available technologies like plumbing pipes for goals, ash for lines and salvaged shade cloth and timber for kiosks.

Playing on Earth

In South Africa's mining and industrial belt, the Witwatersrand, the growth of township football leagues from the 1950s onwards coincided with the development of modernist townships such as KwaThema, built on the 'Rand east of Johannesburg as a segregated dormitory area for black workers. Constructed to a low-density model influenced by post-Second World War neighbourhood planning, with layouts that echoed British New Towns and American suburban tracts, these townships separated rows of houses with buffer strips and skirted the low-lying areas between houses with broad belts of undeveloped space.[5] The open spaces may have appeared as green parks in their planning representations but were underdeveloped during apartheid, and remained as open grassland or just earth. As a *terrain vague*, such township buffer zones had a risky status. While the space itself is a locale for pitches, their definition is lost in the extensiveness of open land and in the overlapping uses that lay claim to it. Football is just one of a series of temporal claims including cattle grazing, farming, car parks, informal housing and religious gatherings.

The power of temporary pitches to maintain spatial agency is clear to the KwaThema grassroots football coach and former Orlando Pirates star goalkeeper, Innocent Mayoyo. Countering ideas of creating World Cup 'Legacy Fields' which invariably led to enclosure, resurfacing, external management and exclusion of some of the current teams, Mayoyo's vision is to promote the game played directly on appropriated earth surfaces. What he calls 'open fields' spring up alongside new social housing developments when new communities instruct the drivers of road graders to clear a field in exchange for a small donation. The open pitches are largely earth, with posts constructed from plumbing pipes or timber. Their access for weekend matches is organised within the community according to consensus between teams, and during the week they are used for practice by boys. The pitches are integrated into their surroundings by virtue of their use as shortcuts through the area, and are protected against invasion for housing.

Mayoyo's understanding of the ephemeral networks of leagues that take place in the township of KwaThema suggests a counter-practice for the support of football that uses only the most direct moves. The leagues and their spaces are a temporal and self-constructed layer of township urbanism that can be seen as a counter-project to the sport's recent commodification and institutional control. The pitches and the players on them are not absolutely separated out from the SAFA network, but nor are they under its control. Some will pass from community to SAFA control and then back to local municipality management, coinciding with their physical transformation through construction and subsequent neglect. Their shifting status is complicated by the interrelationship between the physicality of spaces and their social meaning. If the hallmark of an institutionally owned field is its fencing, then that of a community-owned one is its openness through the lack of fencing. At the same time, the absence of any markers may lead to the loss of recognition of a pitch and its social amenity. Marking pitches more permanently, without enclosing them, might maintain local claims to them.

White Lines
Design interventions in KwaThema's football spaces can amplify a common formal gesture: the placing of a white line on the earth as a way of designating the pitch. The delicacy and deliberateness of this gesture is striking in aerial images where ash lines sometimes stand out. Moreover, the overlay of white pigment onto earth is a very stark and universal medium of representation, with a fundamental materiality capable of eluding any formal tradition of design. Whiteness is associated with Modernist open space, and becomes a neutral tone for the project, open to later signification. But whitening is also associated with African initiation rituals that cover faces with kaolin or flour to render them anonymous.

The first concept for intervention was the establishment of the whitelineunit. The unit would be a small group equipped with the skills and materials to establish a field anywhere, in the most minimal manner, using white paint onto earth and four goal markers. The unit also had the basics for field-side meetings, in the form of a shade structure and a gas *braai* (barbecue). It was run from 2010 by a group of volunteers, the Imvelo Youth Development Brigade, who helped to locate and organise clean-ups of potential fields in KwaThema township. This group formed after a 2007 design-build studio, the KwaThema Project,[6] and extended their park maintenance into line painting and tent construction. In this strategy, their actions of clearing reclaimed the ambivalence of the open spaces and allow for a collective imagination of their redeployment as community space. Clearing was overwhelmingly effective in its impact.

Further volunteers joined them for a collaborative game organised by the Equality Forum, an LGBT group who came together to commemorate Eudy Simelane, the captain of the South African women's football team who was murdered in a hate crime in KwaThema's Riverside Park. The process revealed a number of overlapping agendas for the open space, one of the first township green spaces, dating back to 1951: its claiming for the Eudy match; use as a potential community garden; remaining a relaxation space established by an artist who had saved trees from being cleared and built a circle of seating; giving grazing land for hostel dwellers' cattle and goats; use for worship circles of religious groups; being fenced as a playground; and serving as a dumping ground for uncollected rubbish. The game also reactivated the concrete slabs of two demolished schools on the site, showing them to be an asset with the potential to support new activities there. One of the local businesses that erect tents for ceremonies put one up for the event, showing how quickly the platform could be transformed for football spectating.

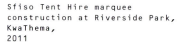

Equality Forum volunteers clearing Riverside Park, KwaThema, 2011

right: As an open space between residential areas, Riverside Park often accumulates household rubbish when the council fails to collect it. By taking on the clean-up by hand, the volunteers, including Msholozi and Portia, precipitated its collection by the council.

Sfiso Tent Hire marquee construction at Riverside Park, KwaThema, 2011

below: Township households use tents for social events like weddings and funerals. They are supported by a vital economy of affordable and efficient home-based businesses renting marquees, chairs, portable toilets and sound equipment.

'Berry 10' shirt drawn on slab
of demolished school building,
Riverside Park,
KwaThema,
2011

above: Two former schools in Riverside Park were condemned due to groundwater, and their brickwork salvaged. Children still play on the slabs.

This event was a first iteration of a generic urban project. In it, football fields would be supported by the design and construction of a thickened edge to the fields, in the form of a strip of support for a mobile shade structure. The materials for the design came from township vocabularies. Specifically, shade cloth and plastic sheeting, including discarded billboards from the FIFA World Cup could be used to create screens, shading and signage. Shade cloth structures typically stand in the zone of ambivalence along the field's street or path edge, sometimes empty, and then filling during a match with spectators, players in waiting, officials and passers-by. They are positioned in between the game and the community at large. Reinforcing them with minimal supports would thicken this zone. Tent anchors made from whitewashed tyres would remain after the match, allowing for the installation of the tent infrastructure for league events, and used for dribbling practices in between. This infrastructure could support three leagues – school, keep-fit and affiliated ones – with the shade structures rotating between them.

Imvelo Youth Development Brigade and Christof van Wyk fixing shadecloth clips for an open pitch tent prototype, 2012

The Imvelo Youth Development Brigade volunteered to put up prototype tents for football. The tents were designed to reuse banners from World Cup advertising.

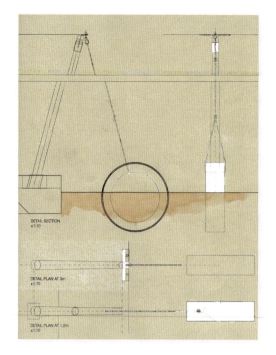

Hannah le Roux,
Sectional drawing through an open pitch tent, 2012

The tents for open fields rely on existing technologies such as used tyres as anchors, gum pole supports, agricultural netting as shading and pipe connections.

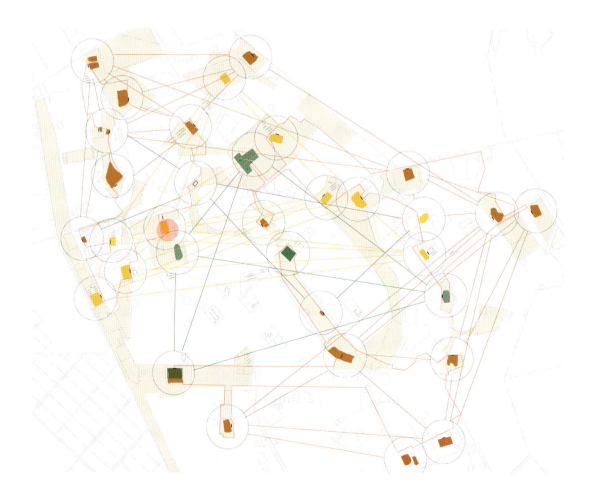

Hannah le Roux,
KwaThema football fields and proposed open pitch league connections, 2013

Pitches are used by different leagues on different days. On tournament days, tents can be put up to shade spectators and additional mobile technologies.

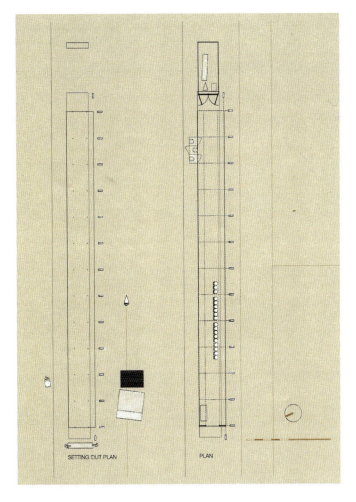

Hannah le Roux,
Plans of open pitch tent set-up and between games, 2012

When pitches are not in use, the tyre anchors remain in place along the edge of the field for dribbling drills.

> When it comes to football, an architecture of refusal can face in two directions: confronting elites who unethically benefited from its globalised upscaling, and supporting communities

Once raised, the edge element could in turn be used by other actors. Additional objects – food stalls, signage, branding and VIP enclosures – could be suspended or housed within its frame, coming both from within and outside of the local township economy. The shade structure and field, and their capacity to change in status between use and emptiness, would become the mediating filters between scales and networks around football and non-football use.

Architecture Against Corruption

The ephemeral nature of open fields makes their impact on football's affective value hard to measure. But their existence, just like that of futsal sites in Brazil and street games around the world, is fundamental to keeping the global game vital. Their presence as a common and uncommodified part of the game challenges the elite circle that manages football on a global scale to be accountable to its followers. In 2015, FIFA was shaken up by the exposure of corruption amongst officials. Its president resigned and now faces fraud charges. Investigations were launched into bribery related to World Cup merchandise royalties, broadcast rights and hosting rights, including a payment of $10 million to Jack Warner, a FIFA vice-president whose vote was significant in awarding South Africa the 2010 hosting bid. It was a fraction of the estimated $3 billion that was spent by the country on hosting infrastructures, including stadiums that now stand empty. The tent project for KwaThema's open fields was put together on a budget of $5,000, one six-hundred-thousandth of the cost of hard infrastructures. These figures suggest that, when it comes to football, an architecture of refusal can face in two directions: confronting elites who unethically benefited from its globalised upscaling, and supporting communities who shape activities and spaces in an ongoing game.[7]

Notes
1. South Africa 2010 Bid Company, 'Africa's Stage: South Africa 2010 Bid Book', South Africa 2010 Bid Company (Johannesburg), 2003.
2. Scarlett Cornelissen, 'More Than a Sporting Chance? Appraising the Sport for Development Legacy of the 2010 FIFA World Cup', *Third World Quarterly*, 32 (3), 2011, pp 503–29.
3. Author's interview with Ekurhuleni Executive Council member, 2011.
4. Peter C Alegi, *Laduma!: Soccer, Politics and Society in South Africa*, University of KwaZulu-Natal Press (Scottsville), 2004.
5. Hannah le Roux, 'Designing Kwathema: Cultural Inscriptions in the Model Township', *Journal of Southern African Studies,* 45 (2), 2019, pp 1–29.
6. Hannah le Roux, 'The Kwathema Project: Designing Negotiations between Planning and Violence', in *The Politics of Design: Proposal Call by IfG, Ulm* 8, unpublished document, Johannesburg, 2007.
7. This text is an edited excerpt from the author's unpublished PhD thesis 'Lived Modernisms: When Architecture Transforms', KU Leuven, 2014. The author's research in KwaThema receives support from the National Research Foundation of South Africa.

Text © 2022 John Wiley & Sons Ltd.
Images © Hannah le Roux

A Cottage to Breathe In

From Bessie Head's House in Serowe
3/4 July 2019

Frangipani
Bloemhof Community Centre

Geranium
Protea Par

Ilze Wolff

Refusing Museums, Making Homes

Ilze Wolff,
Collage image of writer
Bessie Head and her friend
Bosele Sianana in the Boiteko
communal garden in Serowe,
Botswana,
c 1968

Writer Bessie Head, born in South Africa and exiled to Botswana in the mid-1960s, focused particularly on how the loss of the people's land was brought about. Her work is important in understanding the legacies of colonial exploitation and violence in Southern Africa and elsewhere, put in place by the actions of Cecil John Rhodes and others.

Rhodes Cottage is a house-museum dedicated to the life of Cecil John Rhodes – imperialist, mining magnate, politician and former Prime Minister of the Cape Colony in South Africa. **Ilze Wolff** is a co-director of Wolff Architects, who were recently commissioned to make a future-looking strategy for the site and its buildings within this politically loaded historical context.

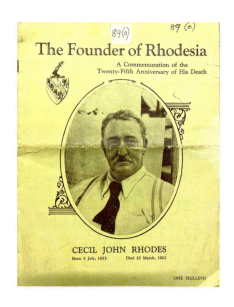

Cover of a 1927 pamphlet commemorating the 25th anniversary of Cecil John Rhodes's death

As part of the commemorations, some renovations were carried out on the house after it had stood empty and boarded up for nearly 10 years.

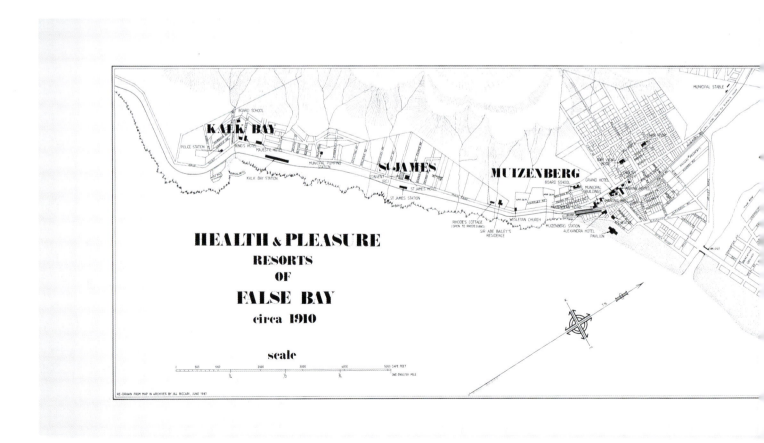

The best way I can explain it is in the words of an industrial millionaire who used his money to conquer the interior of Southern Africa. His main area of conquest – and he waged two wars against the people – was Zimbabwe which formerly had his name, Rhodesia. When he waged the last war of conquest in 1896 he said: 'I have taken everything from them but the air.' The problem is more acute in South Africa. You look across the land as a black person and you feel choked. You feel like even the air has been taken because so many vast areas have been reserved for white occupation only. There's nothing there for black people.

— Bessie Head, during a radio interview in Adelaide, Australia, 1984[1]

Rhodes Cottage is a modest, but stately, sea-facing property along False Bay in Cape Town. It is a house-museum dedicated to the life of Cecil John Rhodes, the industrial millionaire who the South African writer Bessie Head speaks of in the opening epigraph of this article. Rhodes was a British mining magnate and politician in southern Africa who served as Prime Minister of the Cape Colony from 1890 to 1896, and the cottage once formed part of his large estate – an estate that included the University of Cape Town, Groote Schuur Manor House (now the presidential home) and Kirstenbosch Gardens. He acquired the house as a holiday cottage in 1899 in Muizenberg, an area which at that time 'consisted of a few farms and a number of fishing huts'.[2] The timing of Rhodes's purchase and his use of the house coincided with the South African War (also known as the Boer War) that unfolded between 1899 and 1902, in part as a consequence of the failed Jameson Raid instigated by Rhodes and his compatriots in 1895. During the war, Rhodes spent time in Muizenberg and he was soon followed by other mining magnates who built extravagant colonial-style seaside villas. Despite owning other more expansive properties in Cape Town, he chose this humble cottage near the Atlantic Ocean 'because of access to the fresh air'[3] which he needed to recover from a lifelong medical condition that affected his heart and lungs. He spent his final weeks in the front bedroom of the cottage with an 'oxygen cylinder by his bed', and requested his aids to 'knock a hole in the wall of his bedroom opposite the window to allow a through breeze'.[4]

Map of the False Bay area, Cape Town, c 1910

left: As the map's 'Health & Pleasure Resorts of False Bay' label suggests, at the turn of the 20th century the area became increasingly rescripted as a site of leisure and recuperation, thus moving out of an era dominated by coastal industries such as fishing and whaling. The presence of Rhodes Cottage, in a way, gave material form to this rescripting and so a number of other wealthy politicians and mining magnates began developing the area with elaborate seaside villas.

Rhodes Cottage in 1953 functioning as a public museum dedicated to Rhodes

below: In 1953, 100 years after Rhodes's birth, the cottage was permanently converted into a public museum, opened by the Mayor of Cape Town. Filled with relics associated with Rhodes's life curated and selected by an appointed committee, it would function to develop a public culture around Rhodes's colonial legacy, his affiliation with De Beers Gold Mining and also display the images of his 1902 funeral procession to the Matopo Hills in Bulawayo.

Various details of the aftermath of his death – such as how the South African government obeyed his request for his remains to be transported by train from this house to the Matopo Hills, southeast of Bulawayo, Zimbabwe, just over 2,000 kilometres (1,200 miles) away, stopping at every major city along the way for mourners to pay respect; and how, since the railway line stopped short of that destination, it was extended by black Zimbabweans as the procession was underway – are contained in the house itself, expressed in triumphant terms. Neither these nor any other details are framed to viewers as a critique of the violence that Rhodes represents. Nowhere in the house do you find for instance the song 'Cecil Rhodes', composed by Hugh Masekela and recorded on the 1976 album *Colonial Man*. Nor do you find any books by Dambudzo Marechera, a Zimbabwean writer who grew up in 'Rhodesia' under Ian Smith's regime in the 1950s and 1960s and then with cutting precision described the colonial situation in his books *Black Sunlight* (1980)[5] and *House of Hunger* (1978).[6] These and other sources are largely missing in the house. It is as if the house itself is a stuffy, damp vault that sits outside but simultaneously next to some of the most socially transformative uprisings against the legacy of Rhodes – the #RhodesMustFall movement – that were instigated by students at South African universities in 2015.

In mid-2021, Wolff Architects were appointed by the City of Cape Town to develop a conservation management plan (CMP) for the Rhodes Cottage. The scope of the work included writing a statement of significance based on the site's history, and developing an action plan to cover its management in terms of public safety, conservation and education. The task, in other words, was to outline how this building should be managed for public use. In order to do so mindfully and creatively, it was first necessary to gain an understanding of the building and its historical presence. Knowing what there is to know about Rhodes, through student protests and the work of Bessie Head – an important southern African writer and freedom advocate of the 1960s–80s – meant that the approach could *not* be politically neutral. The report would need to carve out a new future-present: a new story for this space as we continue to live in the afterlives of slavery,[7] colonisation and apartheid.

The Caretaker's Cottage

On our arrival in June 2021, three buildings were found to be in fairly good condition: the main cottage, a coach house and a small two-room structure called the caretaker's cottage. There were many photographs of the main cottage as part of the museum exhibition and in the City of Cape Town archives. These photographs show the house as Rhodes found it – a dilapidated, corrugated-iron-roofed house with an unruly stone wall and wooden fencing – and then its transformation after his death into the neat, thatch-roofed house of today. Hans Fransen's *The Old Buildings of the Cape* (1980) gives some information on the house prior to Rhodes's purchase. In a fleeting description of the neighbouring property, Fransen writes: 'The oldest part of the house is thought to have been built as a fisherman's cottage'.[8]

The condition of the house upon Rhodes's purchase, c 1899

By the time that Rhodes purchased the cottage, the original thatch roof had been replaced with a corrugated iron one and a long verandah had been added to the front of the house. After his death, his architects reconstructed the thatch roof, increasing the pitch of the gable to accommodate a steeper slope. The two dormer windows were removed in the process.

Other historical sources are more telling of the area's history and why it is completely plausible that the foundations of the house would be those of a fisherman's cottage. In 1742 Simon's Bay, the town 16 kilometres (10 miles) away from the cottage, became a permanent winter anchorage for the Dutch, meaning cattle were kept constantly on site. It was militarised with the construction of protective fortifications built to protect against outside attack. Indigenous and other local inhabitants built structures for living and storing fish and lived off natural resources such as seafood and fresh water. Aggressive Dutch colonial claims for land for settlement and trading resulted in conflict with local communities, including the 1795 battle of Muizenberg. Local indigenous and creole soldiers were coerced into fighting against the British in order to remain in political and commercial control of the land. The Dutch failed and the British succeeded in seizing the land, with no consent or permission from any of the other major communities that lived, worked and stewarded it and its resources before any settler arrivals. Up until the 1834 abolition of slavery, the various European settlers under colonial British rule constructed infrastructure with the labour of enslaved people of various descent (enslavers forcibly brought people from Indonesia, Sierra Leone, Mozambique and Angola). Ex-enslaved Muslim people worked freely as fishermen and women in the area, later joined by Filipino migrants in the 1850s. A mosque built in 1846 on Quarterdeck Road is an architectural testament to the Muslim fisher community of the time; and similarly the 1858 Catholic Church in St James to congregants of Filipino descent. The cottage adjacent to Rhodes Cottage contains remnants of a fisherman's cottage from about 1856. These remnants may very well be what is today referred to as the 'caretaker's cottage', on the far corner of the site.

The Report and the Pushback

With this information in hand, work proceeded quickly, and the report that followed both provided a practical

The beginnings of the Main Road, c 1844

Prior to the railway line and Rhodes's purchase of the cottage, the houses along Main Road, Muizenberg were used to accommodate enslaved people, freed slaves and Filipino fishermen, roughly between 1844 and 1870.

View of Muizenberg Beach near the Rhodes cottage, c 1904

Fishing boats, cottages and fishermen's storage huts on the beach. The image captures the context within which the cottage existed during the time that Rhodes occupied it up until his death in 1902. The 'caretaker's cottage' on the Rhodes Museum site today would have been in service of accommodating migrant fishermen from the Philippines, freed slaves and descendants of enslaved people. None of this history is currently included in the museum displays.

maintenance schedule and illustrated a shift in the ethics around the narrative of the space. In 1938 the cottage was donated to the City of Cape Town by the Rhodes Trust. The deed of transfer stipulated that the building would function as a museum in perpetuity, a condition that was welcomed and gladly accepted at the time. The current building and site is dominated by the history of Cecil Rhodes, who lived there between 1899 and his death in 1902. The building and immediate site is over 200 years old and the report proposed a broader, more inclusive retelling of its history. This history includes that of enslaved people, working-class black, brown and immigrant histories, and histories from beyond the borders of Southern Africa. As an ethic of engagement, this was largely approved by the City of Cape Town, yet the museum curators, the Muizenberg Historical Conservation Society (MHCS), heavily opposed the report, submitting an 11-page document undermining and contesting it on the grounds that its purpose is to 'delegitimise the property and to [sic] that Cecil Rhodes should be erased completely'.[9] MHCS also contest that Wolff, as heritage architects, should be neutral, that the perceived activism slant is 'unprofessional', that the references to the various settler colonial regimes are 'disparaging remarks aimed at nothing more than the cancellation of white society' and that a paragraph on the urban context is 'viciously anti-white'.[10] The research on the presence of enslaved people's histories were, in their opinion, 'emotive'.[11] Finally, they claimed, in reference to the fact that indigenous societies roamed and occupied the landscape, that: 'The Khoi were largely extirpated by smallpox by the middle of the 18th century and their migration routes were lost to them. In sociological terms, they were displaced by a more powerful society.'[12]

Some pushback was anticipated but the extent to which it would reveal certain parts of society's passion for denying historical spatial violence was an unwelcome surprise. It reinforced the fact that a constant effort is required to refuse and question dominant histories of place and to offer renewed insights that are simultaneously practical, conceptual and imaginative. This engagement affirmed the need to embrace the 'unprofessional' nature of certain tasks in order to invoke change. Ultimately, these working understandings rely on a continuous search for ways to broaden the 'profession' as architects beyond the construction of buildings but also towards the construction of social cohesion and spaces of freedom.

Returning to a Space of Breathing

> Come and see my home. It's anyplace where nobody gives orders. Tread softly – the walls breathe peace …
> Deep, dark, black peace and the wind don't blow.
> — Bessie Head, 'My Home', published posthumously[13]

In February 2022 the report was approved by heritage authorities: a success in that major decision-makers believe in the revised ethic that the report proposes. The challenge still remains, however, as to how this space can become a marker for an emancipatory spatial practice, a space that 'breathes black peace'[14] rather than a space in which one feels compelled to knock holes in the walls in order to shift the energy and release the air that dampens the 'senses and perceptions'.[15] Rhodes bought this cottage, and chose it as the place for him to heal from a debilitating respiratory condition. Today the space continues to have the incredible potential for healing and to return as a place for breathing. Its history as a public institution further increases this potential to enact healing on a societal and ecological scale. ᴅ

Notes

1. Extract from interview on Radio Adelaide, used with kind permission from the Bessie Head Heritage Trust, Serowe, South Africa.
2. Michael Walker, *Coastal Memories: Muizenberg, St James, Kalk Bay, 1980–1920*, M Walker (Cape Town), 1999, p 10.
3. Charles Shee, 'The Ill Health and Mortal Sickness of Cecil John Rhodes', *Central African Journal of Medicine*, 11 (4), 1965, p 91.
4. *Ibid*, p 92.
5. Dambudzo Marechera, *Black Sunlight*, Heinemann (London), 1980.
6. Dambudzo Marechera, *House of Hunger*, Heinemann (Harlow), 2009 (first published 1978).
7. See Saidiya Hartman, 'The Belly of the World: A Note on Black Women's Labours', *Souls*, 18 (1), 2016, pp 166–73.
8. Hans Fransen, *The Old Buildings of the Cape*, AA Balkema (Cape Town), 1980, p 389.
9. Muizenberg Historical Conservation Society letter, comments of Rhodes Cottage CMP, 2021, p 1.
10. *Ibid*, pp 6 and 11.
11. *Ibid*, p 11.
12. *Ibid*, p 3.
13. Bessie Head, *The Cardinals, With Meditations and Stories*, Heinemann (London), 1993, p 124.
14. *Ibid*.
15. Premesh Lalu, *Undoing Apartheid*, Polity Press (New York), forthcoming.

Text © 2022 John Wiley & Sons Ltd. Images: pp 62–3 © Wolff Architects and the Bessie Head Heritage Trust; pp 64–5 © Courtesy of the City of Cape Town; p 67 © Western Cape Archives and Record Service

A Space of Problems

The Child-Cities of Columbus

COLUMBUS WAS A MAN
COLUMBUS IS A CRATER ON MARS
COLUMBUS IS A MODULE OF THE ISS
COLUMBUS IS A SPACECRAFT SHUTTLE
COLUMBUS IS A MOVIE
COLUMBUS IS A STORY
COLUMBUS IS A BACKSTORY
COLUMBUS IS A POST-RATIONALIZATION
COLUMBUS IS AN OPERA
COLUMBUS IS A PRIZE
COLUMBUS IS A TV NETWORK
COLUMBUS IS A SAUSAGE COMPANY
COLUMBUS IS A BIKE FRAME
COLUMBUS IS A NETWORK
COLUMBUS WAS A BUS SYSTEM
COLUMBUS IS A MOB SCULPTURE
COLUMBUS IS A CRUISE SHIP
COLUMBUS IS PROPERTY
COLUMBUS IS IN THE US NAVY
COLUMBUS IS COMMUNITY
COLUMBUS IS A DAY
COLUMBUS IS VIOLENCE
COLUMBUS IS A COUNTRY

Jennifer Newsom and Tom Carruthers

Dream The Combine,
Columbus is …,
2021

Research for Dream The Combine's exhibition uncovered a pluriverse of Columbuses – including places, people, products, positions and times.

Columbus is a STATE
Columbus is a PROVINCE
Columbus is a PERSON
Columbus is a FAMILY

Columbus is a FIRST NAME
Columbus is a LAST NAME
Columbus is a STREET
Columbus is an AVENUE
Columbus is a HIGHWAY EXIT
Columbus is a TRAFFIC CIRCLE
Columbus is in GEORGIA, ILLINOIS, INDIANA, KANSAS, KENTUCKY, MINNESOTA, MISSISSIPPI, MISSOURI, MONTANA, NEBRASKA, NEW JERSEY, NEW MEXICO, NEW YORK, NORTH CAROLINA, NORTH DAKOTA, OHIO, TEXAS, WISCONSIN (TWICE)

*Columbus is an INHERITANCE
Columbus is an PROJECT

Jennifer Newsom and Tom Carruthers are architects, artists and co-founders of creative studio Dream The Combine. They describe their recent artwork/landscape intervention in Columbus, Indiana, and their attempts to unravel the associations of the town's name, its colonial legacies and rich histories of marginalised communities and their contribution to the culture of the place as a microcosm of American social politics.

Alan VanNahmen, *Discover Columbus!*, Columbus, Indiana, 2004

Linking Christopher Columbus and the so-called 'Discovery' of the Americas, this welcome sign to the modern-architectural haven of Columbus, Indiana simultaneously operates as a touristy catchphrase and a facile entanglement of colonial violence.

> Your perception of their connectedness is correct: They have the same infrastructure, the same culture, the same hungers and fears. Each city is like the other cities. All of the cities are, effectively, one city. This world, in this now, is the city's name …
>
> — NK Jemisin, *The Stone Sky*, 2017[1]

Approaching Columbus, Indiana, at the intersection of Interstate 65 and State Road 46, lay a landscaped sign enthusiastically encouraging you to 'Discover Columbus!' The sign's message links Christopher Columbus's efforts 'discovering the new world' to the world discovering this small city in Middle America. To an outsider, the sign was notable for how its catchy slogan facilely encased legacies of imperialist violence. Many in the town did not immediately see a problem with the association, as Columbus (the man) has often been a stand-in for bravery, curiosity, newness and, of course, discovery. Who would not want these virtues associated with their town and used as a driver for tourist dollars? Yet the underlying malignancy of these shallow associations was a thread that Dream The Combine wanted to unravel.

The sign harkens back to the 15th-century papal decrees that established the Doctrine of Discovery. These documents – including the Dum Diversas, the Romanus Pontifex and the Inter Caetera – endorsed the slavery of non-Christians and gave exclusive and total right to lands encountered through exploration to the empires who found them, in disregard of the long histories of indigenous peoples. The texts fuel the origin myths of manifest destiny used to support genocide, slavery, resource extraction, land theft and its divvying into property – acts still present in our landscape today.

Overwriting and Way-Finding

That those legacies sit alongside many acts of resistance to these trajectories is testament to our human capacity to envision the world differently from what it is. Through the installation *Columbus Columbia Colombo Colón* (Columbus, Indiana, 2021), Dream The Combine aimed to portray the complexity of this overlapping web by moving through and moving otherwise to sanctioned history. Geographer and sound artist AM Kanngieser notes, 'The immensity of the loss of people and ecologies to capitalist brutalities exceeds what we can comprehend. But as Indigenous and Black Studies scholars,

artists, and ecologists show, so do the myriad, and insuppressible flourishing and alliances, the joyfulness and love, the lives lived otherways.'[2] That we can find a way through the everyday reach of violence is an important counter to our involute history. We can attune ourselves to the silences of loss, and, in turn, promote our blooming.

'Columbus' is both a physical place (in Indiana and elsewhere), and a system of signification extending in every direction. Its ubiquity has rendered it imperceptible for the simple fact that it has seeped into everything around us. Columbus and his derivations are present in the names of a bus system, a movie studio, a fraternal order and a sausage company, among many others. To trouble this normativity, Dream The Combine researched dozens of places named for the Italian explorer. By entering into dialogue with the mythologies Columbus inspired, the multiple histories in these locales are disquieted. These globally distributed sites and their stories were then transposed as a series of 20-foot (6-metre) tall vertical markers in the physical landscape of Mill Race Park in Columbus, Indiana. Similar to the ways in which past expositions and exhibitions have presented a miniaturisation of the world, the installation consisted of 58 flagpole-like props without their flag-images, each corresponding to a specific place named Columbus, Columbia, Colombo or Colón.

Dream The Combine,
Columbus Columbia Colombo Colón,
Columbus, Indiana,
2021

Aerial view of the entire installation. The 20-foot (6-metre) tall spin-polished aluminium poles cohere with other infrastructural markers that lend metre and time to the landscape: flag poles, lampposts, telephone poles, etc.

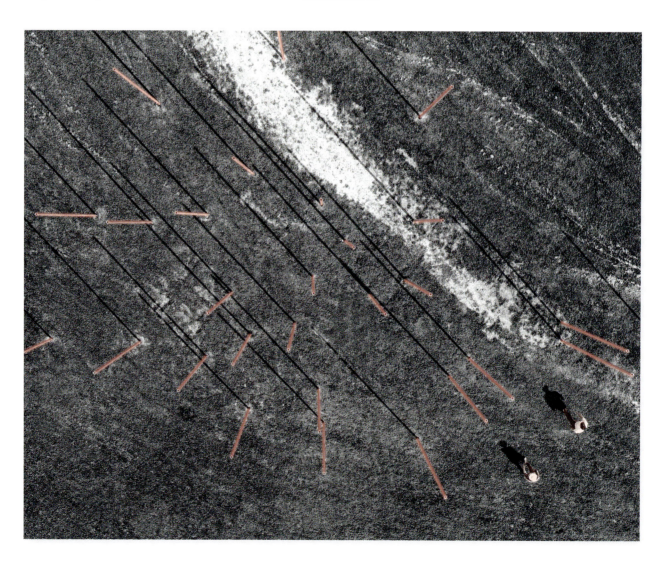

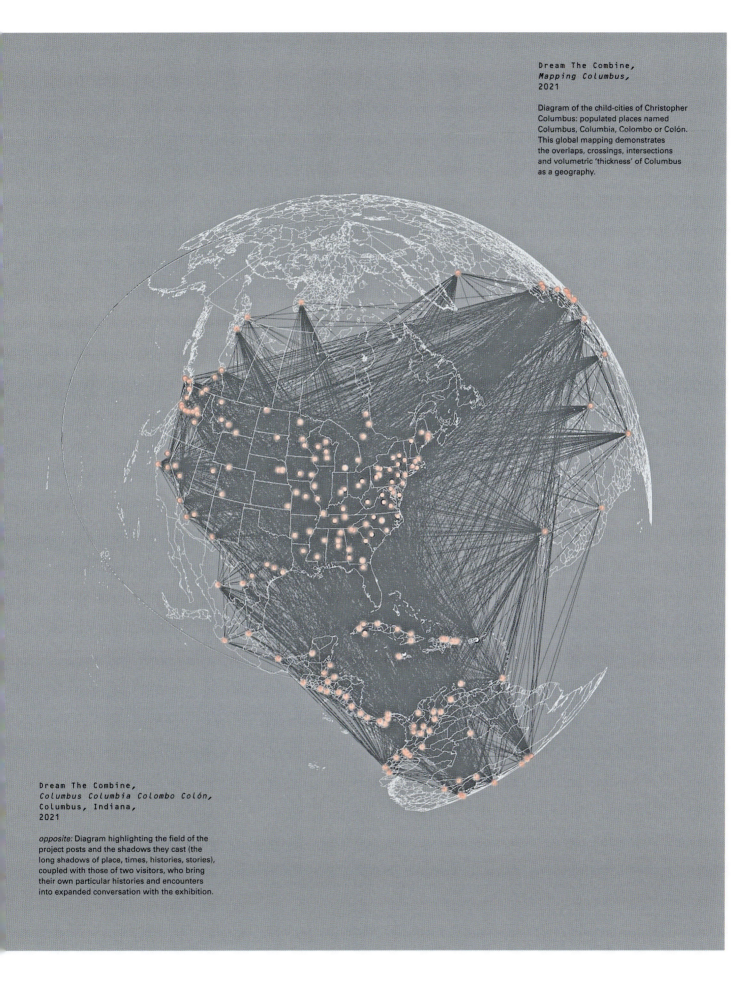

Dream The Combine,
Mapping Columbus,
2021

Diagram of the child-cities of Christopher Columbus: populated places named Columbus, Columbia, Colombo or Colón. This global mapping demonstrates the overlaps, crossings, intersections and volumetric 'thickness' of Columbus as a geography.

Dream The Combine,
Columbus Columbia Colombo Colón,
Columbus, Indiana,
2021

opposite: Diagram highlighting the field of the project posts and the shadows they cast (the long shadows of place, times, histories, stories), coupled with those of two visitors, who bring their own particular histories and encounters into expanded conversation with the exhibition.

Poles were arranged using the cartographic projection developed by 16th-century Flemish mapmaker Gerardus Mercator and in use during the Age of Exploration. Mercator projection flattens the sphere of the Earth to a cylinder, allowing sailors to use straight lines, also known as rhumb lines or loxodromes, to plot connections between points on the globe. While, on the map, angular positions and alignments are maintained, visually the spacing of horizontal parallels compresses the size of objects at the equator and enlarges them as you move away from it, likewise skewing perceptions of the dominance of European colonial powers in the scope of human history. These compass headings fuelled the 'discovery' of new lands; here Dream The Combine's installation reclaims this way-finding system to move between implicated and entangled histories. The method of mapping connects each pole relationally to that of its siblings. If you stand at the pole for Columbus, Indiana and face the one for Columbus, Montana, for instance, following that rhumb line would take you to that new location, collapsing the larger world and the installation upon one another.

Each pole has a spiralling thread of text on its surface which includes an alphanumeric code for Columbus (A#), Columbia (B#), Colombo (C#), or Colón (D#), the place name and country, the date when this naming occurred (as opposed to 'founding'), and a partial history, recipe, quotation, song lyric or other narrative fragment that contextualises or refers directly to that place.[3] Navigation through this textual 'image' is an overwriting of established networks – both a necessary palimpsestic elaboration and a political act. Visitors thus embark on a 'grand tour' of uniquely constructed stories, where reading induces a dizzying, spiralling movement. The texts become embodied via the inner ear. The applied text was cut into long film strips from reflective aluminised Mylar which, when placed on the spin-polished aluminium poles, moved the text in and out of awareness. From a distance, it is not perceptible; as you move closer to the installation, the lettering emerges from its buffed surfaces.

The work constructs a spatial imaginary, stretching frames of reference and probing the deep section of territory. The material extends rigidly from the ground like a lightning rod, but unlike artist Walter de Maria's *The Lightning Field* (1977), the composition is not uniform in its distribution. The poles are all the same height, and their scattershot arrangement takes advantage of the section. From the top of the hill, the eye grazes the tops of the lower poles, as though surfacing from an ocean. Their depth into the earth is a mystery. The poles are densely placed, some as close as 3 feet (1 metre) from one another. They form an intensive field condition that seems enclosing yet has no beginning or end. You know when you are inside it even as it has no edge.

The work resists image so that the text on its surface can form a new imaginative picture.

Reconstructing Past and Present

Eighty per cent of the narratives referred to black, indigenous and people of colour, 26 per cent referred to white people, and 14 per cent referred to nature or land. (Totals exceed 100 per cent as many narratives referred to multiple populations.) Over

Dream The Combine,
Columbus Columbia Colombo Colón,
Columbus, Indiana,
2021

opposite: Detail of the Colombo, Sri Lanka pole. The spiralling text – a poem by Sri Lankan poet Jean Arasanayagam comprising aluminised Mylar lettering wrapped around one of the exhibition's aluminium posts – is foregrounded against a train car from the Louisville and Indiana Railroad.

right: The project is in direct engagement with the mythology of 'the city on the hill'. Here the photograph emphasises the fabricated nature of the terrain that the exhibition is inserted within, imbricating the emancipatory and reckoning nature of Dream The Combine's work.

below: A view from another vantage point of the grounds illustrates the seemingly 'natural' slope of the landscape and the posts ascending towards its peak.

10 per cent were in a language other than English, including Spanish, Portuguese and Anishinaabemowin. Thirty-four per cent were first-person accounts.

They include humorous anecdotes, such as that of musical prodigy John William 'Blind' Boone (Columbia, Missouri, named 1821), pioneer of ragtime music who said his sounds put 'the cookies on the lower shelf for all to enjoy'.[4] Or stories of uplift, such as enslaved and later self-liberated architect Horace King who built a number of important structures in Columbus, Georgia (1828) and Columbus, Mississippi (1819). Some speak to geopolitical conflict, others to resistance to colonial expansion. They span numerous countries, the vestiges of which can be seen from the neighbouring observation tower.

Many places in the United States were named in or after the 1820s, at the height of slavery and during an era of rapid white westward expansion in the wake of the Louisiana Purchase and the Missouri Compromise. The forced removal of indigenous people from their lands (formalised in the 1830 Indian Removal Act) assisted naming practices as white settlers incorporated towns and claimed indigenous lands as their own. As Ojibwe leader Ogemagigido noted at the 1819 signing of the Saginaw Treaty near what is now Columbiaville, Michigan (named 1857), 'Your people pass upon our hunting grounds. You flock to our shores. Our waters grow warm; our land melts like a cake of ice; our possessions grow smaller and smaller; the warm wave of the white man rolls in upon us and melts us away.'[5]

It is no surprise these protest narratives repeat over and over – indigenous people continually proclaim their right to exist on their homelands. Indeed, days before printing the last batch of texts, Dream The Combine found a statement by the Penobscot Nation, issued in July 2021 in response to a replica of one of Columbus's ships being launched in the Penobscot River near Columbia Falls, Maine (named 1863) as part of Maine's bicentennial celebrations. While the use of this ship was 'offensive in numerous ways as well as historically inaccurate it is also deeply harmful to the Wabanaki Nations as well as the descendants of all Indigenous Nations who live in the lands and waters that our ancestors have been stewards of since time immemorial'.[6] (The pole for this location includes the entire 588-word statement, spanning the pole's length.) Across the continent in British Columbia (named 1858), Arthur Manuel wrote a letter to Pope Francis demanding he renounce the Doctrine of Discovery, citing 'those church doctrines remain, more than 500 years later, the core legal justification for the confiscation of our land and subjugation of our peoples'.[7]

Chorus
This is a story without an ending. Some may say Columbus was the beginning, but really he is a footnote in a long list of white supremacist protagonists. And yet overwriting may prove a potent methodology seeking, as Victor LaValle writes in *A People's Future of the United States* (2019), 'narratives that release us from the chokehold of the history and mythology of the past … and writing that gives us new futures to believe in'.[8] But what if, as scholar David Scott questions, an examination of our past 'no longer serves to guarantee the opening of an emancipated future?'[9]

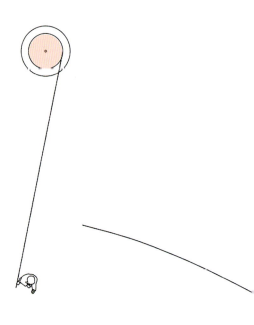

Rather than offering solutions, the installation can be read as a 'a historically constituted discursive space' where one must navigate 'moves in a field or space of argument'

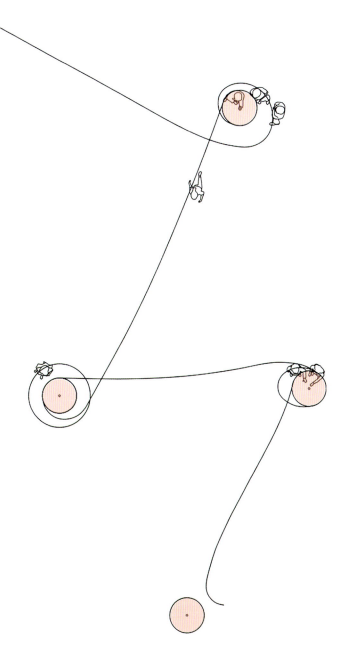

Dream The Combine,
Path and Post Diagram,
2021

As a discursive space, visitors navigate their own entanglements with and paths through the conceptual and physical space of the installation, enhancing the ensemble and sense-making nature of the project.

It is a necessary question.

Rather than offering solutions, the installation can be read as a 'a historically constituted discursive space' where one must navigate 'moves in a field or space of argument'.[10] People moved through this space as partners in an inelegant dance, spiralling and staggering through the landscape of poles, using them to both disrupt and steady their sense of balance. Or, instead of circumnavigating the poles, strangers would stand on either side of one, speaking the visible words out into the air. This out-loud, collective reading moved the work into sound and externalised the written stories as oratory. The chorus implicated the body as a different kind of vessel.

Words from poet Jean Arasanayagam (Colombo, Western Province, Sri Lanka, named 1815), describing the civil war that ravaged her country, take on new resonances. 'Now we are strangers', and we either

> Wait for the release of death
> Or embark upon a ship
> That takes us rootless
> Without maps
> To fare forth
> On a voyage without end.[11]

That we are buoyant demands that we make sense of what we are sailing through. ◙

Notes
1. NK Jemisin, 'Prologue: Me When I Was I', *The Stone Sky*, Orbit (London), 2017, p 12.
2. AM Kanngieser, 'To Undo Nature; On Refusal As Return', *Transmediale*, 2021: https://amkanngieser.com/work/to-undo-nature-on-refusal-as-return.
3. For pole texts and English translations, see: www.dreamthecombine.com/columbus-columbia-colombo-colon-narratives.
4. State Historical Society of Missouri biography of 'Blind' Boone: https://historicmissourians.shsmo.org/blind-boone.
5. Mike Mills, 'Our Land Melts Like a Cake of Ice', 23 September 2019: https://mike-mills.medium.com/our-land-melts-like-a-cake-of-ice-c189af89175.
6. Full statement by the Penobscot Nation: www.newscentermaine.com/article/news/local/penobscot-nation-disappointed-and-disheartened-by-christopher-columbus-ship-replicas-visit-to-bucksport-santa-maria-maine-bicentennial-commission/97-6d7790b3-8ae3-49f9-8302-774d96079cd7.
7. Arthur Manuel, 'Open Letter to Pope Francis', *The Reconciliation Manifesto: Recovering the Land, Rebuilding the Economy*, Lorimer (Toronto), 2016, pp 281–2.
8. Victor LaValle and John Joseph Adams, 'Introduction', *A People's Future of the United States: Speculative Fiction from 25 Extraordinary Writers*, One World (New York), 2019, p xiv.
9. David Scott and Stuart Hall, 'David Scott by Stuart Hall', *Bomb Magazine*, 1 January 2005: https://bombmagazine.org/articles/david-scott/.
10. *Ibid*.
11. Jean Arasanayagam, 'Now We Are Strangers', *Apocalypse '83*, International Centre for Ethnic Studies (Colombo, Sri Lanka), 1984, p 43.

Text © 2022 John Wiley & Sons Ltd. Images: pp 68–71, 72(b), 73, 76–7 © Dream The Combine; pp 72(t), 74–5 Hadley Fruits, Photo Copyright 2021 Exhibit Columbus.

RECLAIM THEIR FUTURE

RIOTOUS RESISTANCE AND INDIGENOUS CREATIVITY IN SOUTH AMERICA'S HIGHEST METROPOLIS

Carwil Bjork-James

Maya Mbaï Mihindou,
Protest en el Cielo,
2022

Alteños march through a landscape filled (from bottom to top) with instruments of road blockades, a rail bridge, a *cholet*, the Teleférico cable-car system and the Cordillera Real of the Andes mountain range. Both *'El Agua es Nuestro, Carajo'* (The Water is Ours, Damn it!) and *'El Alto de Pie, Nunca de Rodillas'* (El Alto on Its Feet, Never on Its Knees) were major slogans of early 21st-century protests.

Assistant Professor of Anthropology at Vanderbilt University in Nashville, Tennessee, cultural anthropologist **Carwil Bjork-James** recounts the recent history of Bolivia and its struggles and ambitions to recognise grassroots ways of occupying its urban fabric. Focusing on the dyad of El Alto/La Paz, he illustrates both mistakes and progress, and shines a light on the ability and tenacity of the country's indigenous and working-class inhabitants to take matters into their own hands through protest and urban interventions.

'Gas War' anti-privatisation protests,
El Alto, Bolivia,
2003

Working together, El Alto residents levered train cars off the rails and onto the street below, turning the privatised and disused vehicles into a barricade during 2003 protests against gas privatisation.

El Alto and La Paz are an urban dyad conjoined at the cliff's edge where the Altiplano (high desert plateau) gives way to the Choqueyapu River valley. While twins in size, El Alto and La Paz are often defined by opposites: wealth and poverty, Creole and Indigenous, officialdom and informality, established power and new arrivals. Overwhelmingly populated by Aymara indigenous people, El Alto is the result of ceaseless tides of inward migration over the last four decades. Former farmers and miners established themselves in neighbourhoods that grew up out of the red-tinted dirt, traced into a variety of miniature street grids of idiosyncratic designs – the diagonal brick patterns of Gran Poder, the hexagonal spiderwebs of Mariscal Santa Cruz. While officially recognised as a city only since 1985, El Alto's population surpassed that of wealthier La Paz shortly after 2000. It fans out from the sprawling La Ceja market across the high-altitude flatlands some 4,100 metres (13,450 feet) above sea-level. There, a monumental scrap-metal statue of Che Guevara looks defiant over La Paz, Bolivia's administrative capital, below.

A Stratified Metropolis in Revolt

Life in this double metropolis is stratified by altitude. Viewed from La Ceja, downtown La Paz is encased in a bowl, with its presidential palace and legislative chambers obscured by the high-rise towers 450 metres (1,470 feet) downhill. Alteños ride minivans and buses down the curving highway, wind down steeply pitched streets with bundles tied upon their backs, or march downhill towards the Plaza San Francisco, La Paz's largest square and the nation's gathering place for working-class protest. Bolivia is one of the most politically mobilised countries in the world, and street protests have helped end over a dozen presidencies in the past century. The highway splits into the two sides of the stately Prado, descends through stylish Sopocachi, and curves down through a canyon. Finally, it enters the modern Zona Sur. Here the thinness of El Alto's atmosphere, the strain of hypoxic exertion and the possibility of a morning snowfall all give way to the warmth of the tropical sun. All the polarities of El Alto and La Paz are played out on this descent, which is also the trunk line of urban mobility.

The main passages out from this capital metropolis are all high-altitude roadways. The routes that form Bolivia's 'economic axis', linking its major cities and allowing foreign trade to Peru, Chile, Argentina and Brazil each begin in El Alto. Poorer but on higher ground, El Alto holds all the vital arteries of the capital in its grasp. At the turn of the century, Indigenous Bolivians realised that they hold this power. Peasant protesters erected scores of road blockades across the rural plains in September 2000, and many Alteños joined their cousins by blocking the main roads through their city. After 26 days, the government conceded to the protesters' demands.[1]

In September 2003, El Alto became the focal point of wider protests against gas privatisation and for a new constitution expanding Indigenous rights. Alteños erected road blockades throughout the city, stopping goods from entering La Paz and fuel from departing the Senkata gas plant. The military cracked down hard on the city, killing at least 46 Alteños. Undeterred, protesters remade urban thoroughfares into barriers to commerce and defensive ramparts against military gunfire. They dug trenches, built walls and toppled metal pedestrian bridges. Hunger-strike pickets multiplied. Less than a week after the military offensive, the president resigned.[2]

The New Politics of Inclusion

A fundamental change in the complexion of Bolivian politics had begun. In 2005, Bolivians elected Aymara coca grower Evo Morales as their first Indigenous president. Morales was once one of just four Indigenous deputies in the legislature. By 2010, the renamed Plurinational Legislative Assembly had 38 Indigenous members (23 per cent). The Indigenous Wiphala was raised alongside the Republican tricolour flag as a new state symbol. These political changes have been matched by moves that remake the city. The emerging pattern? An ethnofuturism in which Andean motifs, Indigenous cultural diversity and informal street culture now shape architecture and infrastructure.

Municipal politicians in the metropolis have had to address the needs of working-class and Indigenous residents, often by redesigning the urban realm and its spaces of circulation. Aymara street vendors, their goods bundled in colourful traditional fabrics, now descend concrete public staircases instead of dusty paths that once turned to mud in the rain. The stairs were built by the La Paz municipal government, along with plazas, health centres and covered basketball courts that double as community meeting sites. These material improvements add a new layer of convenience and dignity.

In the urban core, however, planners' visions have kicked up new conflicts with everyday people. In 2014, planners proposed to 'upgrade' the Garita de Lima roundabout, promoting visual plans which showed no trace of the vendors who inhabit the space: the tarps they string up, the blankets they sit on, their large pleated skirts. Vendor leader Julia Manuela Hilarión was outraged: 'It is by fighting that we have won our vending posts and now we are surprised that they are kicking us out of this place.' On the third day of a collective hunger strike, vendor Teodora Velasco de Quispe died of a heart attack. The myopic project was shelved.[3]

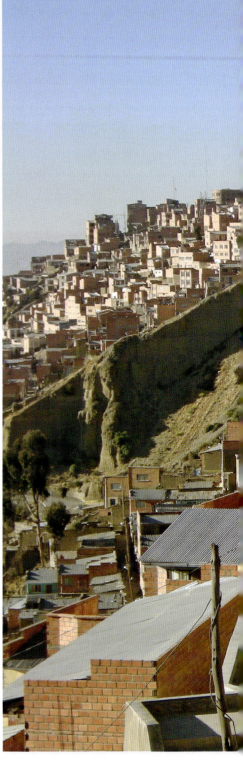

Public walkways and playground, El Alto/La Paz, Bolivia, 2009

Urban walkways and staircases enable dignified navigation of El Alto/La Paz's steep and otherwise muddy slopes. The playground, built in consultation with local residents, features a mural celebrating the 1781–82 Aymara siege of La Paz.

Municipal politicians in the metropolis have had to address the needs of working-class and Indigenous residents, often by redesigning the urban realm and its spaces of circulation

Building an Indigenous Future

The most iconic change to the metropolitan landscape emphatically rejects the opposition between modern and Indigenous: Mi Teleférico is a system of aerially suspended cable cars that spans El Alto and La Paz, carrying 97 million riders in 2019.[4] The premiere public transit project of Evo Morales' national government, Mi Teleférico implanted high-technology infrastructure and rapid cross-town transportation in many working-class communities, while providing incomparable views of the dual city. The towering metal columns that support the system rise out of El Alto's Avenida 16 de Julio, a street filled with vendors and lined by self-consciously futuristic *cholets* built of glass, tile and metal. In downtown La Paz, bright terminal stations jut out of the architectural landscape like alien ships, clad in colourful tiles and flanked by graffitiesque murals. With travel times halved and each station named in the Aymara language, the system has upended the conceptual geography of the city.

Roberto Ameneiro Galdo,
Riosinho Pampa
Teleférico Station,
La Paz, Bolivia,
2017

Clad with colourful tiles, the Mi Teleférico stations insert a hypermodern transportation system into the urban landscape of El Alto and La Paz.

Mi Teleférico cable cars and murals in the Cementerio General, La Paz, Bolivia, 2018

Part of Bolivia's vibrant and often political street art, both commissioned and graffiti murals often complement the cable-car system around El Alto and La Paz.

In the first decade of the 2000s, Alteños showed their willingness to blockade and even tear down parts of their city to make a new Bolivia. The staircases and murals, *cholets* and cable cars show a capacity to reimagine and rebuild that same city. Aesthetically, the emerging Aymara metropolis is unapologetically Indigenous but wildly modern.

Some speculated that the arrival of conspicuous consumption and relative comfort would render El Alto politically dormant. Indeed, the city stirred little when nationwide protests cried fraud over Evo Morales' re-election in 2019. However, when police tore the Wiphala flag off their uniforms, El Alto rose up again. Blockades were erected across the city. Soldiers responded with a fresh massacre outside the Senkata refinery. Alteños once more toppled the pedestrian overpasses to aid in their protests.[5]

After a year of right-wing government, new elections were held in 2020 and 2021. Eva Copa, the outspoken young Aymara senate president, is now El Alto's latest mayor.[6] Political struggles over ownership of the city and the country's natural resources have led to creative endeavours through which the Indigenous and working-class majority claims not just their city, but also the future. A rebellious spirit continues to characterise the city. ⌂

Notes

1. Raquel Gutiérrez Aguilar, *Rhythms of the Pachakuti: Indigenous Uprising and State Power in Bolivia*, tr Stacey Alba D Skar, Duke University Press (Durham, NC), 2014.
2. Forrest Hylton and Sinclair Thomson, *Revolutionary Horizons: Past and Present in Bolivian Politics*, Verso (New York), 2007.
3. Carwil Bjork-James, 'La Paz, Bolivia: Death of a Protester', Carwil Without Borders blog, 4 March 2014: https://woborders.blog/2014/03/03/la-paz-death-of-a-protester/; 'Gremialistas denuncian un muerto en vigilia contra proyecto', *El País*, 14 February 2014: www.elpaisonline.com/index.php/sociales-2/item/116819-gremialistas-denuncian-un-muerto-en-vigilia-contra-proyecto.
4. Mi Teleférico, 'Audiencia Final: Rendición Pública de Cuentas, Gestion 2019', 2020: www.miteleferico.bo/?download=17149.
5. Anatoly Kurmanaev and Clifford Krauss, 'Ethnic Rifts in Bolivia Burst into View with Fall of Evo Morales', *The New York Times*, 15 November 2019: www.nytimes.com/2019/11/15/world/americas/morales-bolivia-Indigenous-racism.html; Anatoly Kurmanaev and Elisabeth Malkin, 'As Violence Grips Bolivia, Congress Moves Toward New Elections', *The New York Times*, 20 November 2019: www.nytimes.com/2019/11/20/world/americas/bolivia-deaths-sentaka.html; Pablo Mamani Ramírez (ed), *Wiphalas, luchas y la nueva nación: Relatos, análisis y memorias de octubre-noviembre de 2019 desde El Alto, Cochabamba y Santa Cruz*, Plural (La Paz), 2020.
6. 'Evo vs Eva: In Bolivian Highlands, a New Political Generation Emerges', Reuters, 4 March 2021: www.reuters.com/article/us-bolivia-election-preview-idUSKBN2AW231.

Aboard Mi Teleférico, El Alto, Bolivia, 2019

A traditionally dressed Aymara woman gazes out of a cable car at a *cholet* on the Avenida 16 de Julio. El Alto has become a centre for Andean ethnofuturism. The term *'cholet'* combines the French *'chalet'* (large house) with *'chola'* (indigenous woman).

Text © 2022 John Wiley & Sons Ltd. Images: p 79 © Maya Mihindou; pp 80–1 © Ali Burafi/Getty Images; pp 82–5 © Carwil Bjork-James

THE ERUV AS LEGAL FICTION

Piper Bernbaum

Eruv markers in Buffalo, New York, 2015

The eruv can enclose different areas of the city for use on the Sabbath, depending on the desires of the community. It will enclose residential areas, but frequently includes recreational spaces such as parks and outdoor areas.

Eruvin often rely on 'tapping into' the city's existing infrastructure in order to build their boundaries. By doing so, they are as non-invasive as possible, while also covering great distances.

CHANGING RULES IN THE PUBLIC REALM

Assistant Professor at the Azrieli School of Architecture and Urbanism at Carleton University in Ottawa, **Piper Bernbaum** finds magic in 'legal fictions', and especially the Jewish eruv. While many legal fictions offer privileges to individuals and create spatial systems of power, the eruv is not exclusive; it includes the existing urban fabric of the city and all its people, and on the Sabbath emancipates the orthodox community to provide an extended domain of domestic space.

An eruv roofline extending near the High Line park in Manhattan, New York, 2015

opposite, bottom left: Eruvin must adapt to the growth and changes in a city. Manhattan's eruv, once the High Line was established, extended itself in order to include the very popular park for its community members to visit on the day of rest. Eruvin are modified frequently in response to the community's needs.

In cities around the world, 'invisible' lines of fishing wire trail through urban neighbourhoods. These are the outlines of Jewish *eruvin*.

An *eruv* (translated: mixing/mingling)[1] is an Orthodox Jewish practice that allows for leniency on the Sabbath (day of rest), to allow people greater ease in managing and adhering to Jewish law.[2] Through the physical construction of a boundary line and the symbolic enclosing of a representatively domestic space, the eruv creates a shared domain in the city that is interpreted as an extension of the home. The establishment of eruvin rewrites the rules of our interpretation of public and private space, allowing the city to become both sacred and intimate. The eruv is adaptive and subtle yet re-negotiates how individuals can use space.

The Evolution of the Eruv

The eruv has existed in practice since the Mishnaic period and was written into the Talmud. However, for thousands of years, it relied upon existing boundaries of city walls and fortifications around urban centres to enclose space. Modernisation of society and the redistribution of the Jewish community during diasporas of the 19th and 20th centuries meant that the eruv was required to evolve with the contemporary city. It emerged as a form of adaptive urbanism to support Orthodox communities, often having to respond to specific group needs and contexts of their built surroundings.

The contemporary eruv is constructed with commonplace materials: 2-by-4-inch (5 × 10 cm) lumber, fishing line, zip-ties, ribbon, plywood, and wood or steel posts. It is generally visually unremarkable; however, in its humble form lies a remarkable power. The contemporary eruv is a reinterpretation of the architectural components required to form a private domain as outlined within the Talmud. Because it is symbolic, there is not one material that is required to fabricate it. What is essential from the interpretation of Talmudic texts is that the components of the household be represented: a wall, a roof and an opening/doorway.

Both physically and symbolically, the eruv allows for an extension of the private domain into the public realm of the city for the duration of the Sabbath. This offers members of the community the affordance to perform bare necessities of daily life as if the city streets were their private household.[3] These actions would otherwise be considered work, and therefore forbidden. For example, a mother can carry her baby to the park, or an individual can push an elderly member of the family in a wheelchair to synagogue or carry medicine on their person. The eruv allows for apparent assimilation, but in fact is a maintenance of tradition. 'Homemade' and nearly invisible, it offers lessons in a specific form of refusal – one that actively redefines the accepted domains of public and private space.

An eruv marker in Manhattan,
New York,
2015

left: One of the most commonly used materials found in eruv construction is fishing line. Used to connect all the components and markers of the eruv (built or appropriated from the city), the fishing line represents a communal roofline under which all citizens and community members dwell freely.

The meeting of eruvin
in Manhattan,
New York,
2015

below right: Eruvin are established through a lease with the city but are managed by the community itself. Often, when there is a sufficiently large Jewish population, it is possible to encounter multiple eruvin meeting or overlapping. As a practice of faith, it is up to the individual to decide if the eruv they require is being properly maintained or not.

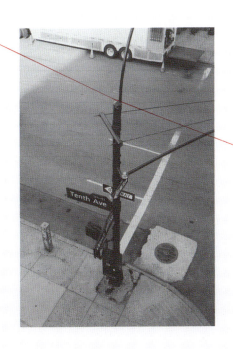

Although the route of the boundary line is fascinating, the eruv's true value is found through its practice of construction: it is built by citizens, with everyday materials, and by assessing existing structures and systems of the public realm

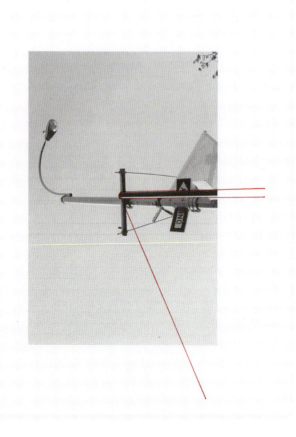

An eruv marker in Kitchener, Ontario, Canada, 2015

above: Eruvin will use various forms of markers, such as 2-by-4-inch (5 × 10 cm) posts, to represent different components of the home and private domain. Depicted is an eruv marker for a *lechi*, or doorpost, zip-tied to the bottom of a telephone post.

An eruv roofline extending from a light post in Brooklyn, New York, 2015

left: Eruvin require an enclosed loop for space to be considered kosher for the Sabbath. If an eruv line ever breaks, it cannot be used for its leniencies on the day of rest. Community members verify eruvin weekly, to make sure they are 'up' and functioning for the Sabbath.

Legal Fiction as Loophole

The eruv is a 'legal fiction' (as defined by the Marcus Jastrow Talmudic dictionary): an assertion accepted as true however likely fictional.[4] As a loophole, it finds ways around the legal structures in place – both in Jewish law and in civic legal allowances. In many ways, the eruv is a placeholder for religious devotion; it allows for forgiveness in practice and provides freedom to live. However, the notion of legal fiction extends beyond religious law. Within the city, the eruv engages with civic policy. Although not explicitly listed in municipal regulations, the eruv space and construction is typically submitted to and approved by a city's planning department. This procedure results in a symbolic lease with the city, allowing for a 'rental' of public domain on the Sabbath. It is the Jewish communities themselves that seek out these permissions and the lease. The transaction empowers the community, legitimises the practice and allows for freedom in the way the community dwells in the city. Through the transaction between Jews and the city (as well as Jews and non-Jews) there is an acceptance and acknowledgement of difference. The eruv's lease is crucial: for the space to be deemed Kosher, it needs to be rented to be considered a privatised domestic space. By leasing the public domain, the community can dwell in the public sphere of the city and treat it as an extension of their family's living room. By engaging with policy and law, the eruv inherently subverts it. It uses bureaucratic systems to justify its existence, but its spatial practice is a commentary on the constraints of civic space. This form of DIY space – an architecture responding to the conditions of the city – is built entirely by the citizens who require it. The eruv (and its legal fiction) is a tool to provide safety within and takes on everyday architectures as a form of citizen-led empowerment.

Legal Fiction as a Form of Urban Practice

Although the route of the boundary line is fascinating, the eruv's true value is found through its practice of construction: it is built by citizens, with everyday materials, and by assessing existing structures and systems of the public realm.

The eruv is an example of a legal fiction within the domain of the city and of the often-overlooked interventions that exist between reality and fiction, legal and illegal space, or owned and shared land. Legal fictions most often exist in figurative discussions and decisions. In formal settings, legal fictions are used by entities to establish control and security: embassies that exist within one country but are owned by another nation, divisions of territories within airports at customs where one room can belong to two countries, international borders between countries, or even bodies of government or businesses that maintain corporate personhood to act as an individual. Legal fictions, in these instances, utilise systems to maintain order and power.

Legal fictions are both figurative and physical. However, they often intentionally go unnoticed. In this sense, the built worlds of legal fictions are only a small portion of the complex and intricate systems upon which they are reacting. Even though the eruv is classified as a legal fiction and deals directly with policy, legal fictions themselves are not as commonly accessible; building them often requires greater resources than are available to the average person.

Because of this, the eruv is a unique example of urban practice. Unlike most legal fictions that come from a place of power and privilege, it is citizen-led, citizen-built and reactionary to the systems already in place in cities. As a spatial loophole, the informal quality of the eruv suggests that everyday architectures can offer subversive tactics for claiming identity in public space. The eruv hints toward empowerment as subversion, encouraging citizens to learn about the systems in which they carry out their lives. Legal fictions can both provide and disrupt, and in the case of the eruv they define a particular community layered within existing contexts and histories.

An eruv marker attached to an apartment building in Williamsburg, New York, 2015

Eruvin can exist at multiple scales. Although the ones that engage with the large public domains are typically run by a community, individual households or buildings can decide with permission to 'enclose' smaller-scale outdoor shared space, such as roads, courtyards or shared alleyways, in order to use the communal space as a private domain.

The Urban Lesson of the Eruv

By merging the public city with the private living room, the eruv acts as a form of refusal, redefining what is accepted within the shared domain of the city. The delineation between inside and outside is blurred, and the plurality of space allows those who use the practice to participate in the city. In addition, those outside of it can engage with a space that is sacred and witness the occupation of space for use beyond the everyday. So, the eruv contributes to the defining of community and an understanding of spatial use. It is evident in many eruvin that public parks or public paths are often purposefully included to provide spaces of leisure and joy on the day of rest. The eruv draws a line around spaces of desire and need – an urbanism that rewrites the boundaries, borders and edges of neighbourhoods and civic space.

    The eruv provides lessons for designers to speculate on other forms of destabilising urban practice that blur the boundaries of sanctioned and unsanctioned, legal and illegal, visible and invisible, public and private. Such practices locate themselves at the intersections of DIY urbanism (practice through convenience and resourcefulness), tactical urbanism (counter practices to the politics of urban space) and established planning policies that embrace loopholes within their legal frameworks. They exist in spaces of ambiguity and opportunity.

    Unlike tactical urbanism, which generally exists as 'guerrilla' architecture in the public realm, the eruv is a threshold condition delineating between spatial dichotomies. Where tactical urbanism is concerned with change and improvements for the greater collective, the eruv seeks ways to offer relief within a system instead of audaciously trying to improve it.

    Understanding the radical refusal the eruv offers regarding the definition of public and private leads us to many questions around empowerment and negotiation – around how individuals can take hold of their built environments, and how we can find slips between the formal and informal. The appropriation of space holds tremendous potential, and cities where individuals take a stake in their contexts offer opportunities for care and responsibility. The eruv looks to the individual for innovation, to counter the narratives around what architecture can be, focusing instead on what architecture should be. In many ways, it is the antithesis of what we understand as a part of architecture in the contemporary world. It is not aesthetic, it is not mainstream and it is not refined; its physical experience is explicitly non-transformative, but it *is* transformative spiritually and socially. It rewrites the rules of how we use space, and what is expected within space, with people taking charge of their own social sphere and community. And, for 24 hours, once a week, the city becomes a holy and sacred space.

    The eruv encourages a complex civic domain and makes room for people. As an architecture of refusal, it offers a reflection on the potentials found in the most

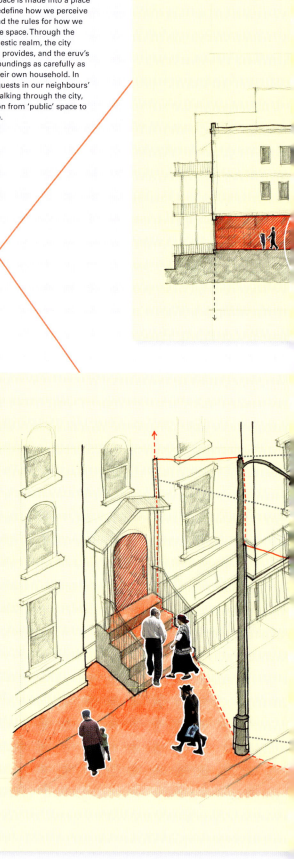

Piper Bernbaum,
The extension of the domestic realm of the eruv into the public street,
2022

Via the eruv, urban space is made into a place of dwelling. Eruvin redefine how we perceive inside and outside and the rules for how we use public and private space. Through the extension of the domestic realm, the city becomes a place that provides, and the eruv's users treat their surroundings as carefully as if they were within their own household. In this case, we are all guests in our neighbours' living rooms when walking through the city, shifting our perception from 'public' space to that of 'shared' space.

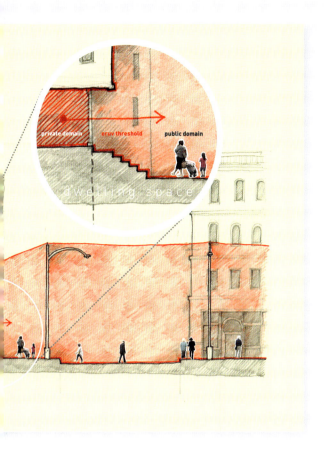

mundane and accessible forms of materials and spaces. There is a vulnerability tied to the existence of the eruv; it asks its community members to take a risk, it seeks permission from the city to share space, and it extends the intimate space of the home out into the common streets for all to share, witness and experience. As a space of appearance, the eruv is a refusal of segregating religious customs, as well as a refusal of obfuscating religious practices and identity in the contemporary city.[5] It is an urbanism of identity and expression – a space built by the everyday citizen for their community. In this unique example, residents and designers are the same.[6]

Above all, the eruv is humble yet bold – often misconstrued as garbage, debris, items, or spaces of neglect. There is magic in the quality of these constructs: through the commitment to making and reacting to our urban environments, a sense of belonging in space is forged. These spaces are underestimated, seen as rough and crude, perhaps even viewed as camp or unattractive. But these constructs express what is desired in space by the people who live in it, not just by the upper powers of the city. This kind of urbanism is a post – it holds place for people and gives opportunity for a voice and small-scale action. The fundamental lesson of the eruv is its central question: Who defines boundaries, and therefore, who has a right to stake a claim to space? ⌂

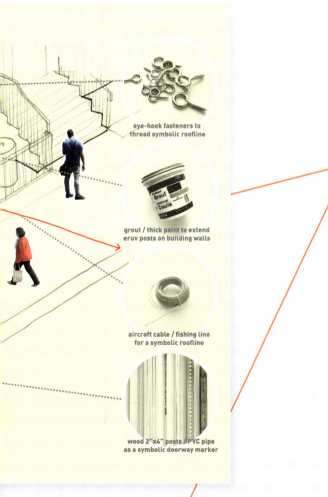

Notes
1. Yosef Gavriel Bechhofer, *The Contemporary Eruv: Eruvin in Modern Metropolitan Areas*, Feldhwim (Jerusalem), 1998, p 1.
2. Michele Rapoport, 'The Intangible Boundaries of the Jewish "Eruv"', *Environment and Planning D: Society and Space,* 29, 2011, p 891.
3. Bechhofer, *op cit*, p 6.
4. Marcus Jastrow, *Sefer Ha-milim: Dictionary of the Targumim, Talmud Bavli, Talmud Yerushalmi, and Midrashic Literature*, Judaica Treasury (New York), 2004, p 1,075.
5. See Hannah Arendt's writings on spaces of appearance in Hannah Arendt, *The Human Condition*, University of Chicago Press (Chicago,IL), 2018, pp 199–211.
6. Mimi Levy Lipis, *Symbolic Houses in Judaism: How Objects and Metaphors Construct Hybrid Places of Belonging*, Ashgate (Farnham), 2011, p 205.

Piper Bernbaum,
The everydayness of eruv materials and forms,
2022

By appropriating space, the eruv marker defines territory through everyday materials. Eruvin are created through a lease in the city, but their physical form and path is defined and proposed by the community itself. Their boundaries can often be guided by available materials, but they will also bend to serve certain buildings or families, or to include specific spaces within their midst. The materials used are so everyday that even a bending eruv line that cuts through streets or connects to buildings often goes unnoticed by the untrained eye.

Text © 2022 John Wiley & Sons Ltd.
Images © Piper Bernbaum

Thompson Cong Nguyen

From Altars to Alterity

Offerings and Inheritances for Queer Vietnamese Kin

Thompson Cong Nguyen,
Hybrid Collage of Grandma's Altar Room in Haiphong,
'Offerings and Inheritances for Queer Vietnamese Kin',
MArch thesis project, Azrieli School of Architecture
and Urbanism, Carleton University,
Ottawa, Canada,
2021

Hybrid drawing of Thompson's grandmother's altar room, using personal photographs taken by the author, sketches of the floor plan drawn from memory, and flash cards of glossary words handwritten in Vietnamese.

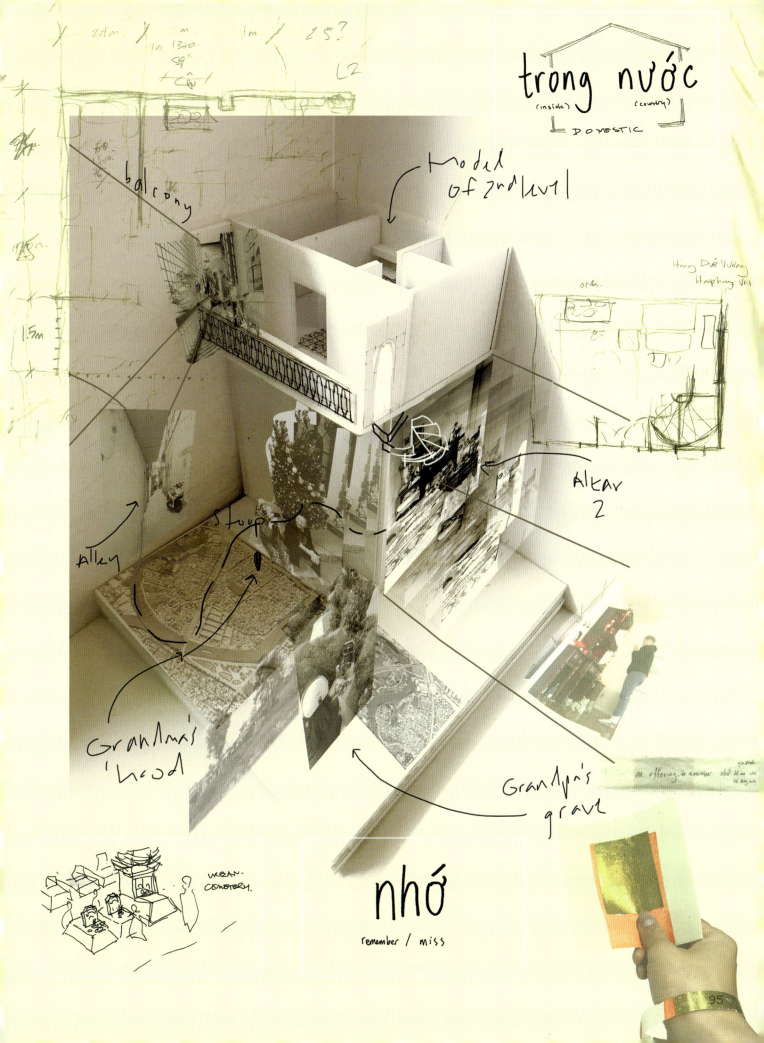

As a child of Vietnamese refugees who settled in suburban Mississauga in Ontario, Thompson Cong Nguyen describes his hybrid cultural identity, queerness and complex inter-relations with the historic ritual of his ancestors and the divergent manifestations of Canadian society. He does so through the design of the set of transportable altars that were part of his MArch thesis at the Azrieli School of Architecture and Urbanism at Carleton University in Ottawa.

How do we offer our selves – as queer, diasporic, Vietnamese families in settler-colonial Canada – to honour our ancestral kinship ties while creating space for new, authentic rituals and traditions? 'Offerings and Inheritances for Queer Vietnamese Kin', my architectural thesis at the Azrieli School of Architecture and Urbanism at Carleton University in Ottawa investigates how practices of ancestral worship are performed in everyday sites scaled to the body, the street and the nightclub. This involved multi-modal and multi-scalar artistic explorations of offerings and identities which prompted the design of three new altars fitted to a suitcase, an urban storefront and a queer clubbing event. Each altar offers new fields of inquiry that embrace the mess of queer diasporic identities and affects how space is conventionally created through architectural design. This process invites designers, scholars, and queer, diasporic kinfolk to collectively reconstruct new practices of belonging for our ancestors, kin and our multi-adjectival selves.

Returning Home from the Altar and Cemetery

In 2016 I visited several cemeteries with my parents and extended family in their home city of Haiphong, Vietnam. As one of the first in my generation born overseas in Canada, I was introduced to several ancestors buried in gravesites across Haiphong's urban core and periphery. As we arrived at each ancestral shrine, we stopped to perform rituals and give gifts as offerings in exchange for spiritual protection. We visited relatives from five generations before us, cleaning their shrines, burning paper money and incense, putting fresh flowers into vases, refilling small porcelain cups with fermented rice spirits, and replacing empty plastic dishes and bowls with fresh fruit.

This was a familiar practice for my cousins, who were born in Vietnam and practised these daily rituals of care. Growing up in suburban Mississauga – close to Toronto – my siblings and I observed altar practices for ancestor worship, but we did not actively participate in them. Ancestor veneration was something my parents saw as their responsibility to uphold, and they did not actively impart this knowledge to their children. Not knowing how to continue these traditions brings me a sense of guilt and loss. From this experience, I sought to

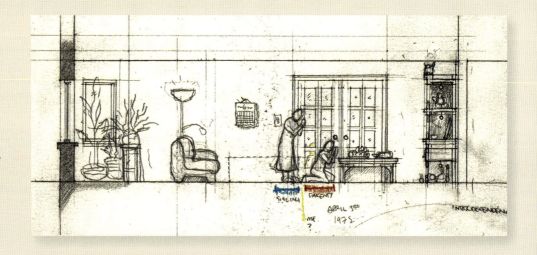

Thompson Cong Nguyen,
Section of Mom and Dad's Altar Room in Mississauga,
'Offerings and Inheritances for Queer Vietnamese Kin',
MArch thesis project,
2021

Sketch of Thompson's parents praying upon their ancestral altar during Lunar New Year. Their altar is placed along the back wall of the room and houses photographs to honour his late paternal grandparents. In Vietnam, the altar is a common fixture in most family homes. In Mississauga, this altar room orients the suburban, immigrant home as 'oriental.'

reconcile how to appropriately honour my parents, siblings and loved ones when they pass on.

As a queer and diasporic person, I want to resist ideals imparted through heteronormative Vietnamese and Confucian patrilineal traditions. Yet still, when reflecting on my relationship to my identity, family and the dead, many questions and desires surface: Who will be responsible for continuing altar practices when these traditions were never taught in my family? If it is me, then how do I make space for altar practices in my daily life? How would I continue these lines of tradition, as a queer, diasporic architect-in-training in settler-colonial Canada? Essentially, what can I offer and how do I do it right?

Offerings, Altars and Identity-making
What is an offering? Is it limited to the ancestral altar and the urban cemetery, the Vietnamese nation and diaspora, or do offerings and exchanges exist everywhere in our everyday lives? What are the intimately spatial and systemically urban characteristics that make these exchanges possible? How do offerings build collective identities and maintain shared place-making? These inquiries pushed me to look to the ancient and recent past to understand what altars and offerings mean to me today.

Offerings are donated physical things or actions, used to strengthen the relationship between descendant and ancestor. This can take the form of giving fruit, burning paper money, or replacing flowers on the altar or shrine. And although rituals to honour the dead were practised in Vietnam for millennia, what we know today as ancestral worship was a result of reappropriated Chinese civil religion.[1] As a facet of Chinese imperial statecraft (as well as Vietnamese state-forming[2]), venerating ancestors upon home altars *(Bàn Thờ)* has been practised within households in Vietnam and across the diaspora for centuries. Through repeated acts and offerings, collective Vietnamese identities are formed through individual altar practices.

Queer and diasporic identities can skew or twist the conventional trajectory of traditional altar practices. Both identities are a result of displacement: diasporic people are displaced from their countries of origin and queer people are often displaced from the reproductive, heterosexual nuclear family unit. To paraphrase Sara Ahmed's 2006 text *Queer Phenomenology*, the rituals and traditions that are inherited in 'familial and social space' are 'oriented' to new lines, fields and potentials because of queerness 'failing' to follow these norms and migration causing us to be 'disoriented'.[3] We must make our own practices.

Thompson Cong Nguyen, *Grandma's Altar and Grandpa's Grave in Haiphong, Vietnam*, 'Offerings and Inheritances for Queer Vietnamese Kin', MArch thesis project, 2022

Thompson's grandmother's altar room in Haiphong on the left and an image of his late maternal grandfather's gravesite to the right, both photographed in 2016. Routes between these sites of ancestral worship and the markets to pick up gifts were embedded into the daily lives of descendants in the city.

Altars allow us to hold multiple timelines and directions in a space we can return to. In this way, altar-making is already a queer and diasporic practice: they are queer as they form our identities in parallel or opposition to dominant normative regimes (such as heteronormativity, model minority narratives or Western religious practices), and they are diasporic through repeating and duplicating practices across histories and geographies.

As diasporic individuals, we must negotiate multiple ways of looking: to reflect on the nostalgia of returning home and to face forward while settling ourselves elsewhere.[4] I consider the altars as offerings and as sites of duty and tradition, while still being a space where queer, diasporic Vietnamese identities could be re-imagined in new forms. What is offered and exchanged, and how? The following three altars explore my personal forms of offering scaled to the individual, the city and the collective.

Altar of the Body: Personal Baggage Tolerances

The first 'Altar of the Body' is contained within a suitcase I found while studying in Ottawa. I customised the suitcase to fit my personal altar objects. My photographs, books, drawings, models, and incense and joss papers have arrived, lived, and will be leaving with me during my studies at Carleton. It is modified with tolerances to tightly fit delicate, permanent altar objects in transport. Ritual items that change frequently are designed with a looser fit.

The queer, diasporic body must constantly address aspects of constraint and tolerance within spaces of everyday life. Fitting my personal altar within the generic dimensions of the hard-shell suitcase unloads the burden of migrating and moving through space, as a queer, Vietnamese designer. This suitcase is a portable, non-permanent altar allowing for a grounding, non-linear temporal custom-fit place made for my kinship ties. How will my suitcase altar connect and transform my own rituals of honouring my families, wherever I go?

Altar of the Street: Columbarium on the Corner

The 'Altar of the Street' embeds collective grief into civic infrastructure. At the intersection of Yonge and Wellesley Streets in downtown Toronto, this altar proposes a columbarium and a public artefact exchange centre at this prominent street corner to make visible the loss of queer, diasporic communities being policed, displaced and forgotten in the city.

The columbarium programme runs along the east façade and the three northern bays of the retail podium, lit by a porous storefront. Cloudy, translucent glass panels wrap around the building's façades, with entryways to invite patrons at the corner of the intersection. In the interior, rows of stackable and shared altars can be accessed by dedicated community members. As altars are in use, glass panels on the exterior elevation will change colour and opacity.

The second programme component, titled the 'Memory Exchange Centre', is a shared community archive. Items that commemorate community members can be held or borrowed by visitors to bring back to their home altars. Suitcases, bags and boxes of items are collected, stored and exchanged.

Thompson Cong Nguyen, *Altar of the Body: Elevation*, 'Offerings and Inheritances for Queer Vietnamese Kin', MArch thesis project, 2022

Collage of a 1:1-scale drawing of a found suitcase and photographs of Thompson's movement and use with the object. The suitcase was designed for modifications as his personal altar to honour his family ties.

Thompson Cong Nguyen,
Altar of the Body: Plans and Inventory,
'Offerings and Inheritances for
Queer Vietnamese Kin',
MArch thesis project,
2022

Sketch of Thompson and a diagram of all of the items he plans to store within the suitcase for his altar practice.

Thompson Cong Nguyen,
Altar of the Street: Hybrid Drawing on Yonge Street,
'Offerings and Inheritances for Queer Vietnamese Kin,
MArch thesis project,
2022

Collage overlaying an isometric drawing, photographs of physical site models, elevations and cue cards of words in Vietnamese and English that make up the Altar of the Street. This altar is an urban intervention at 8 Wellesley Street East, an intersection near Toronto's Church-Wellesley Gay Village.

99

These two public programmes question how we can make a community's shared loss visible in the city. What happens when we centre ritual as exchange along storefronts? How can the urban block become an offering or altar for citizens?

Altar of the Club: A Homecoming Dance
The final altar, the 'Altar of the Club', is an animated collage that embodies the migrations, rituals and practices explored on a night out with queer Asian kinfolk in Toronto. Layering drawings, photographs and videos of queer family dancing, edited to the beat of an iconic 1970s Vietnamese funk track, it pieces together parts of everyday movements of friends and family heading to a fictional Lunar New Year club event for queer and Vietnamese people.

Queer club event organisers have been reclaiming, remixing and reconstructing traditional holidays of East and Southeast Asian culture for decades, but it has taken new forms in the age of social media. Multidisciplinary, design-savvy artist collectives such as Bubble_T in New York, New Ho Queen in Toronto, and the House of Rice in Vancouver output new visual, sonic and electrifying events for contemporary queer, Asian and diasporic urban youth.[5] Organisers of these events have been known to find kinship and production design influences from many collectives led by queer, trans, black, indigenous and people of colour (QTBIPOC) in other cities, such as Papi Juice in New York, and even Club Quarantine online.[6]

Thompson Cong Nguyen,
Altar of the Street: Plans,
'Offerings and Inheritances for Queer Vietnamese Kin',
MArch thesis project,
2022

The film strip depicts Thompson placing a layer of tracing paper down on the plan drawing filmed on camera. The single enlarged plan drawing shows a floor plan with tracing paper and acetate layered on top. In the full-length video, cut-out scale figures, furniture pieces and shared altar niches built on the plan drawing are filmed to consider the many possible transformations of this street corner for collective grief and exchange.

This altar provides multiple ways of looking in plan, elevation and perspective, moving across multiple sites of everyday exchange tuned to a psychedelic Vietnamese rock and soul track. The song, titled 'Con Tim Và Nuóc Mǎt' ('Heart and Tears'), was performed by the CBC Band – a Vietnamese rock band active in Saigon prior to 1975. Hearing the Vietnamese language to the drums, guitar and reverb transports listeners, within and outside of the Vietnamese diaspora, to a time and place of longing. I place myself in the ritual sequence from the pre-party to the coat check, to the dancefloor, and to the post-party recovery meal. In this choreography, one moves to, from and through spaces of community and celebration.

How might working within the conventions of ritual and practice, such as in the motions to celebrate and dance, create new iterations of offerings for our communities?

Inheriting and Honouring Alterity

These explorations in diaspora, queerness and belonging offered me a space to understand how inheritances and altars change across material and spatial scales. We find, collect and make our own altars or altar-like spaces in our daily lives. Altars can be made available to anyone, which can be very powerful for individual bodies, collective families and the public. The altars I encountered in my life provided a deeper understanding of the rituals and the labour required to maintain them. This design labour to honour my families of blood and choice is my offering.

An offering takes something from you, which is something you must be willing to part with. In this exchange, something changes and transforms. As what I offered changes me, I develop a spatial practice that deeply considers the dimensional tolerances, (in)visible infrastructures, as well as the shared grief and joy of my community and family.

Through this intimate investigation on kinship, cultural lineage, sacral and secular traditions, we can collectively discover what spaces emerge when we return to, reject and reconstruct identities for our ancestors, kin and ourselves. In future iterations of this work, I wish to continue making space for grief and celebration – as I believe this is how we honour all that we inherit. △

Notes

1. Alexander Woodside, 'Territorial Order and Collective-Identity Tensions in Confucian Asia: China, Vietnam, Korea', *Daedalus*, Summer 1998, pp 195–200.
2. Heonik Kwon, *After the Massacre: Commemoration and Consolation in Ha My and My Lai*, University of California Press (Berkeley, CA), 2006, pp 1–10.
3. Sara Ahmed, 'Introduction', in *Queer Phenomenology: Orientations*, Duke University Press (Durham, NC), 2006, pp 1–23.
4. Martin F Manalansan IV, 'Migrancy, Modernity, Mobility: Quotidian Struggles and Queer Diasporic Intimacy', in Eithne Luibhéid and Lionel Cantú Jr (eds), *Queer Migrations: Sexuality, US Citizenship, and Border Crossings*, University of Minnesota Press (Minneapolis, MN), 2005, pp 146–60.
5. Sissy Nein, 'New Ho Queen: Together Forever', *Sticky Rice*, 2 (13), November 2020: https://stickyrice-magazine.com/Volume02-New-Ho-Queen.
6. Harvard GSD, 'Black in Design 2021: "Black Matter", Designing for Black Queer Pleasure, Joy, and Intimacy', October 2021: https://youtu.be/kCPvWtkjM80.

Thompson Cong Nguyen, Altar of the Club: Plans, 'Offerings and Inheritances for Queer Vietnamese Kin', MArch thesis project, 2022

Stills from an animated collage presented as part of Thompson's final thesis. They depict the choreographed sequence of queer friends and family arriving at a fictional Lunar New Year 'homecoming' dance. Illustrations of multiple sites of gathering for the queer Asian community are overlaid with photographs and videos collected by Thompson on various nights out with friends in Toronto.

Text © 2022 John Wiley & Sons Ltd.
Images © Thompson Cong Nguyen

101 WAYS TO REFUSE A WALL

Chat Travieso

AN INSTRUMENT OF CONTAINMENT, SUBDIVISION, OWNERSHIP OF SPACE, COLONISATION, AND RACIAL AND POLITICAL DIVIDE, THAT MOST UBIQUITOUS OF ARCHITECTURAL TOOLS – THE WALL – CAN ALSO BE DÉTOURNED, REAPPROPRIATED, DEMOLISHED AND RE-ADORNED. ARTIST AND DESIGNER, AND CO-FOUNDER OF MULTI-DISCIPLINARY PRACTICE YEJU & CHAT, CHAT TRAVIESO LOOKS AT DIFFERENT WAYS OF SUBVERTING THE FUNCTION OF A WALL AS A BARRIER BY EITHER DISREGARDING IT, APPROPRIATING IT, CIRCUMVENTING IT OR ABOLISHING IT, AND THE POLITICAL IMPLICATIONS OF THESE ACTIONS.

The Berlin Wall,
Germany,
28 December 1989

A boy with a hammer and chisel at a graffiti-covered section of the wall. The graffiti, as well as the act of chiselling into the wall, are examples of the 'disregard it' tactic.

In her essay 'Architectural Exclusion: Discrimination and Segregation Through Physical Design of the Built Environment', legal scholar Sarah Schindler states that 'architecture itself is a form of regulation'.[1] While we may interpret our surroundings as innocuous and apolitical, Schindler reminds us that 'By structuring our relationships, these features of the built environment control and constrain our behavior.'[2] Indeed, architecture literally dictates how one can and cannot traverse and access space. It follows that architecture has the power to discriminate and exclude. And unlike discriminatory laws, architecture is solid, tangible, visible.

There is no clearer embodiment of this than a wall. Not only do walls physically contain, keep out, separate and obstruct, they also act as blunt symbols of division and hostility. Oftentimes, they reinforce already existing racist, xenophobic and classist policies and practices, as in the case of race walls built throughout the US to segregate Black and white neighbourhoods, or border walls such as the one separating the US and Mexico.[3] Such barriers further entrench the colonialist belief that people have the right to claim, own and subdivide the earth's surface.[4] Serving as 'the first line of intimidation', these structures demarcate spatial boundaries that if crossed subject offenders to the violence of vigilantes or the punitive carceral system.[5] Moreover, by restricting people's freedom of movement, walls inflict physical, social and psychological harm in themselves – exacerbating existing inequalities by depriving communities equal access to goods and services.

Yet every day, humans devise ways to refuse such forms of architectural control as the ubiquitous fence delineating private property to massive border walls fortifying nation states. If architecture is a form of regulation, its refusal is a form of civil disobedience. Such actions subvert the function of a wall as a barrier by either disregarding it, appropriating it, circumventing it or abolishing it. While sometimes related and overlapping, each of these categories operates differently and has distinct political implications.

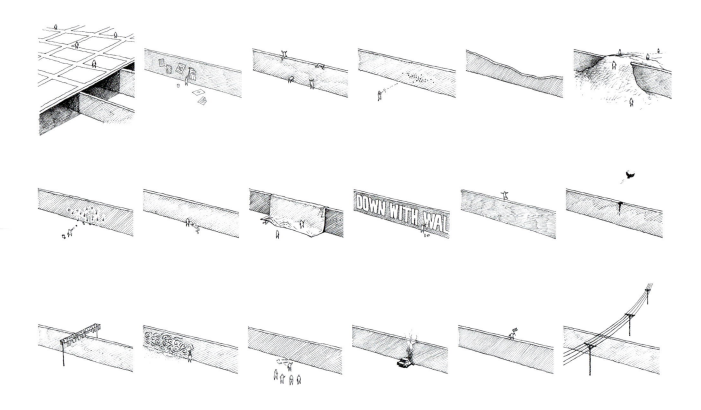

DISREGARD IT

Chat Travieso,
Disregard It,
'101 Ways to Subvert a Wall'
drawing series,
2016

Drawings illustrating ways to disregard a wall.

In 1961, the German Democratic Republic began to build a wall to stop dissatisfied citizens defecting from East Germany to the Western Bloc. Over the nearly three decades of its existence, West Berliners covered their side of the Berlin Wall in graffiti. These political slogans, words of solidarity and public artworks not only decried the subjugation and division the wall enabled; they also disparaged the authority it represented. The same can be said of the West Bank wall today. Like the Berlin Wall in its day, the West Bank wall, which the Israeli government began to erect in 2002, is plastered in words and drawings denouncing how it further isolates Palestinians. Each of these messages is a mark of rebellion.

These acts of vandalism are instances of the 'disregard it' category. This tactic is provocative, irreverent and anti-authoritarian. It recalls the iconoclasm that philosopher Peter Sloterdijk describes in ancient Greek kynicism: 'Ancient kynicism begins the process of "naked arguments" from the opposition, carried by the power that comes from below. The kynic farts, shits, pisses, masturbates on the street, before the eyes of the Athenian market. He shows contempt for fame, ridicules the architecture, refuses respect, parodies the stories of gods and heroes.'[6] Similarly, the 'disregard it' approach repudiates the rules and customs established by built space. To disregard a wall might mean to deface or vandalise it, to throw food at it, to damage it, to urinate or defecate on it, to ignore it, to bury it, to build over it, to misuse it.

Stoop sale, Brooklyn, New York, 2013

far left: Clothes for a stoop sale hanging off the retractable gates outside a closed doctor's office. The adaptation of the gates into a clothes rack is an example of the 'appropriate it' tactic.

Outdoor living room, Brooklyn, New York, 2013

left: An ad-hoc gathering space transforms a chain-link fence and sidewalk into an outdoor living room. The repurposing of the fence for this social space is an example of the 'appropriate it' tactic.

Chat Travieso, *Appropriate It*, '101 Ways to Subvert a Wall' drawing series, 2016

Drawings illustrating ways to appropriate a wall.

APPROPRIATE IT

It is a Sunday morning in Brooklyn, New York, and the doctor's office on the ground floor is closed. There is a stoop sale going on in front of the building. The retractable gates covering the storefront windows and door of the doctor's office have been reclaimed as clothes racks. Five blocks away, there is an ad-hoc outdoor living room. On the sidewalk are several chairs, a table, an armoire desk and a barbeque grill. Tied to a chain-link fence is a camouflage-patterned tarp that functions as the wallpaper and ceiling to this intimate gathering space.

As these everyday examples illustrate, the 'appropriate it' tactic is resourceful, clever, creative and informal. It recognises the latent potential of everything and how our surroundings can be endlessly adaptable. It rejects the intended use of an object or space, and supplants it with new ones. It is the hack it/make-do tactic – appropriating what is already there as a support structure to respond to people's everyday needs.

To appropriate a wall might mean to build off it, such as attaching seats, canopies, solar panels, swings, bookshelves, banners or shelters to it; or to use it in an unexpected way, for example converting it into a rock-climbing wall, a projection surface or a divider for a game of tennis or volleyball. While this tactic aims to transform an object of exclusion into something different, it does not radically upend the status quo and as such can be reformist (rather than revolutionary) in nature.

CIRCUMVENT IT

The 'Ridglea Wall',
Fort Worth, Texas,
1969

Sign in the Como neighbourhood, part of the 'Ridglea Wall'. Como youth dug a hole under the fence to reach jobs on the other side in Ridglea, an example of the 'circumvent it' tactic.

A sign posted on a 10-block-long, barb-wire-topped fence in Fort Worth, Texas, declares 'NO TRESPASSING KEEP OUT'. The fence, erected in the late 1940s to keep Black residents in the Como neighbourhood from entering the affluent white area known as Ridglea, blocked access to doctors, dentists and shops into the 1970s.[7] Taking matters into their own hands, Como youth dug a hole under the so-called 'Ridglea Wall' so that they would not have to walk all the way around it to get to their jobs. As a community member recalls, 'we'd go down to the hole and slip under, my cousin and I'.[8] They would then go to the country club in Ridglea where they worked as caddies. After work, they would crawl back under the barrier to return to their homes in Como.

Whether out of necessity, as the above example highlights, or as a show of rebellion, the 'circumvent it' tactic is about outsmarting and finding loopholes. It evades authority and surmounts obstacles. To circumvent a wall might mean to get past it by going under, over, around or through it; to steal something from the other side, like fruits from a tree or Wi-Fi; or to build connections with the other side, whether they are physical, social or visual. This tactic is defiant, cunning and aspirational. By making a mockery of the wall's function of separating, it seeks to underscore the absurdity and moral deficit of division.

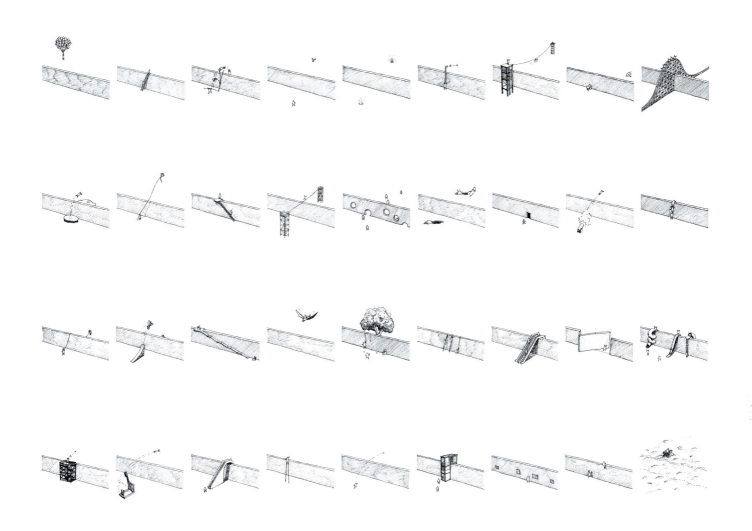

THIS TACTIC IS DEFIANT, CUNNING AND ASPIRATIONAL

Chat Travieso,
Appropriate It,
'101 Ways to Subvert a Wall' drawing series,
2016

Drawings illustrating ways to circumvent a wall.

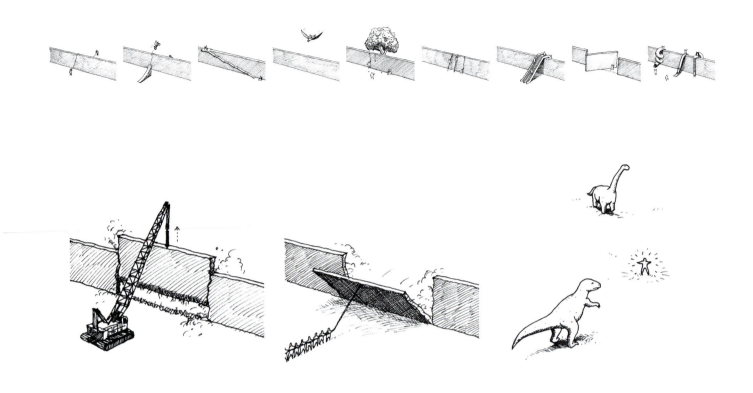

ABOLISH IT

Chat Travieso,
Abolish It,
'101 Ways to Subvert a Wall'
drawing series,
2016

Drawings illustrating ways to abolish a wall.

In December 1962, the then mayor of Atlanta, Ivan Allen Jr, ordered the construction of wood barricades across Peyton and Harlan Roads to keep Black Atlantans from accessing the white neighbourhood of Peyton Forest after a Black surgeon named Dr Clinton Warner purchased a home there. The action was met with strong opposition from Atlanta's civil rights groups. Protesters formed picket lines around the barrier, deeming it 'Atlanta's Berlin Wall', and immediately filed lawsuits in local courts. But as told by historian Kevin M Kruse, some activists went further. They 'pulled the I-beams out of the ground, sawed the timbers in half, and tossed the scraps into a nearby creek'.[9] After white residents restored the roadblocks the next day, 'raiders returned and set fire to the new barricade'.[10] Eventually, a judge ordered the barricades be removed, 72 days after they were originally erected.

The activists who destroyed the roadblocks embody the 'abolish it' ethos. This tactic is revolutionary and militant. It sees no value in preserving unjust institutions and seeks to obliterate existing power structures rather than work with them or elude them. Instead of succumbing to despair, it is active and strong-willed. To abolish a wall means to not only physically wipe it out by blowing it up or tearing it down; it is also about eradicating the social, political and economic systems that constructed it to begin with.

'Atlanta's Berlin Wall',
Atlanta, Georgia, 1963

A barricade dubbed 'Atlanta's Berlin Wall' constructed to keep Black Atlantans from moving into the white neighbourhood of Peyton Forest. Activists attempted to destroy the barricade, an example of the 'abolish it' tactic.

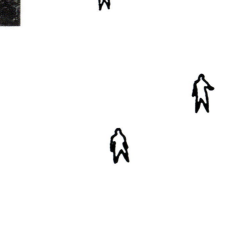

NEVER BUILD IT

Chat Travieso,
Never Build It,
'101 Ways to Subvert a Wall'
drawing series,
2016

Drawing illustrating the 'never build it' tactic.

In a time of rising authoritarianism worldwide, it is easy to surrender to a sinking sense of despair. Yet moments of architectural refusal (as the ones outlined above and others) offer hope. As Michel Foucault reminds us, 'no matter how terrifying a given system may be, there always remain the possibilities of resistance, disobedience, and oppositional groupings'.[11] In their dissent against injustice and control, such acts as disregarding, appropriating, circumventing and abolishing walls introduce an insurgent glimpse of new possibilities in which all forms of containment (such as borders, prisons and private property) are eradicated. In short, a future in which walls (both physical and metaphorical) are never built again.

NOTES

1. Sarah Schindler, 'Architectural Exclusion: Discrimination and Segregation Through Physical Design of the Built Environment', *Yale Law Journal*, 124 (6), April 2015, p 1,943.
2. *Ibid*.
3. For more on race walls in the US, see Chat Travieso, 'A Nation of Walls', *Places Journal*, September 2020: https://placesjournal.org/article/a-nation-of-walls/?cn-reloaded=1.
4. Reinhold Martin, Jacob Moore and Susanne Schindler (eds), *The Art of Inequality: Architecture, Housing, and Real Estate*, Temple Hoyne Buell Center for the Study of American Architecture (New York), 2015, p 20.
5. Chat Travieso, 'Concrete Terror: Race Barriers and Vigilantism in the United States', in Germane Barnes and Shawhin Roudbari (eds), *MAS Context, Issue 33: Vigilantism*, 2021, p 239.
6. Peter Sloterdijk, 'Critique of Cynical Reason', *Theory and History of Literature*, 40, University of Minnesota Press (Minneapolis, MN), 1988, p 103.
7. Travieso, 'A Nation of Walls', *op cit*.
8. Brazos Film & Video/1 Square Mile TV, *The Fence Between Rich and Poor – Fort Worth, TX (Lake Como)*, 24 October 2010.
9. Kevin M Kruse, *White Flight: Atlanta and the Making of Modern Conservatism*, Princeton University Press (Princeton, NJ), 2007, p 4.
10. *Ibid*, p 5.
11. Michel Foucault, 'Space, Knowledge, and Power', *Foucault Reader*, ed Paul Rainbow, Pantheon Books (New York), 1984, p 239.

Text © 2022 John Wiley & Sons Ltd. Images: p 102 © Jill Stoner; pp 104–5, 107–8, 109(r) © Chat Travieso; p 106 ©The University of Texas at Arlington Library Special Collections; p 109(l) © Kenon Research Center at the Atlanta History Center

Cathy Smith

MEAN BOD

ARCHITECTURE WITH

Cathy Smith,
Meanwhile Bodies,
2022

Detail section. Bodies and architectural vessels in perpetual motion. As cities struggle with the confluence of health, economic and environmental challenges, it is time to acknowledge the meanwhile bodies these conditions produce, negatively or otherwise.

WHILE IES

OUT PROPERTY

The meanwhile use of properties provides a quick fix for the problems of urban blight and wasted building assets, but we also need to better consider the experiences of those who temporarily occupy them. Australian architect and Senior Lecturer in Interior Architecture at the University of New South Wales in Sydney, **Cathy Smith** explains the concept of 'meanwhile' and illustrates some of the spatial opportunities that can be used to momentarily ease the precariousness that some of the world's populations find themselves in.

When considering what has been denied or refused by architecture (and thus what needs to be returned to the discipline), it is important to acknowledge those meanwhile, temporary or nomadic bodies that have been historically underrepresented or excluded from its practices and discourses. In every moment in the present world, there are scenarios producing meanwhile bodies that temporarily inhabit, produce and consume global cities. Whether through climate change, economic precarity, warfare or various combinations thereof, these bodies do not rise and fall in cities in any synchronised way. Bodies become displaced, economies collapse, cheap housing is in short supply while buildings remain dormant. The lives of these meanwhile bodies are dynamic, complicated, ambivalent and sometimes unsettling, and therefore infrequently discussed in the mainstream and popular media. In response, the images of inhabited meanwhile spaces shown here simultaneously refer to and undermine architectural conventions, thereby capturing messy lived urban realities produced through an equally messy and experimental drawing process of layering and intermixing analogue and digital imagery.

The meanwhile bodies of current focus are those with temporary property tenures that preclude them from longer-term residence in a specific building or wider neighbourhood. Whether by choice, forced circumstance or both, these meanwhile bodies increasingly dominate our urban milieus. Skyrocketing property prices in global cities from London to Sydney have made property unaffordable even for professionally qualified workers. Many, if not most people now live in buildings they do not own, possess or control with any certainty, effectively operating as building custodians on behalf of their property owners (whom they pay to secure temporary shelter).

above: External elevation. Joyously experimental and insecure in equal measure, meanwhile bodies problematise the way we think about and represent architecture and the city.

below: Detail elevation. The unpredictable, dynamic and at times precarious urban occupations of meanwhile bodies resist the static formalist design approaches and representational imagery that dominates popularist architectural media.

Even in a developed global city like London, financially vulnerable populations are forced into less reliable but cheaper property tenures across a spectrum that ranges from private renting or leasing through to the monthly rolling licenses of residential 'property guardianship' and its 'live-work hybrid'.[1] As implied by the tenure's namesake, property guardians temporarily 'guard' or occupy vacant, submarket urban buildings, typically until the properties are requisitioned by their owners for upgrade or future redevelopment.

Initially conceived in the Netherlands as a form of 'anti-kraak' or 'anti-squatting'[2] to discourage the unauthorised occupation of vacant buildings, UK property guardianship is posited as a legitimate property 'sector'[3] in its own right, because it addresses the twin problems of vacant buildings and rising property unaffordability. There, it is also marketed as a form of urban regeneration that involves the temporary insertion of creative start-ups and community activities into buildings and neighbourhoods slated for redevelopment: from underused and dormant buildings, former schools, hospitals and warehouses through to decanted housing estates. Schemes are administered by third-party, typically for-profit guardianship and meanwhile-use providers who use bespoke short leases or monthly rolling occupation licenses. Advocates of property guardianship see it as a necessary remedy for individuals and sites in transition that exists alongside but does not supplant permanent accommodation solutions. In an ideal scenario, a meanwhile scheme provides access to quality, affordable shelter for those demographics who would otherwise be financially precluded from accessing it. Those schemes involving architects and professional designers have resulted in quality spaces for their meanwhile communities[4] – but this is not always the case.

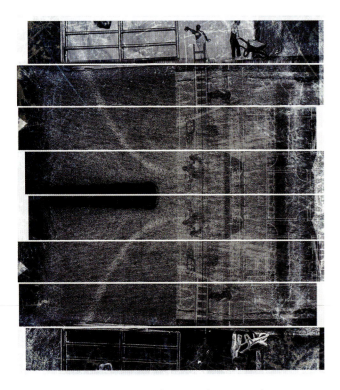

Plan. Once considered an expression of grassroots, impromptu action, meanwhile use has become a tool of mainstream urban planning.

Converting vacant commercial and institutional buildings into inexpensive temporary housing is neither easy nor uniformly embraced, as satirised in the fictional UK television series *Crashing* (2016).[5] Set in an abandoned hospital, one of the more memorable though disturbing scenes involves a near-miss electrocution in a decrepit bathroom. The submarket condition of some guardianship buildings like the one featured in *Crashing* prompts interesting comparison to London's historical residential squatting. Some guardians see paying to occupy submarket condition buildings as akin to 'commodification' of squatting. To quote from event manager and head guardian 'Kate' in Episode 1 of *Crashing*: 'I'm not a squatter, OK, I do pay.'

Irrespective of whether property guardians are celebrated as the cultural saviours of derelict neighbourhoods or derided as the naysayers of impending gentrification, they are as vulnerable to property market conditions as the communities they replace, despite their employment and education. As such, the plight of these ordinary working citizens highlights the extent and widespread impact of the property affordability crisis. Given their significance within contemporary cities, why are meanwhile bodies so rarely discussed or represented in architectural discourse?

Internal elevation. The duration and presence of meanwhile bodies in particular buildings and neighbourhoods is highly dependent upon factors beyond their control, from the desires of individual property owners to the flows of global investment capital.

Site plan. Visualising the temporality and indeterminacy of urban meanwhile bodies is difficult, but necessary, to render visible their contributions to urban form.

REPRESENTING (IM)PROPRIETY

Planning for and representing meanwhile bodies has been historically difficult in architecture, not least because their occupations challenge foundational Western concepts of property and place, particularly those entangled with tenure security, social longevity and material durability. Architectural discourses have historically paid scant attention to the systems of property and land ownership that precede the construction of architecture and built form.[6] Perhaps property ownership is so deeply embedded in Western culture that it is accepted as given with any architectural commission: indeed, the accumulation, possession and control of property have also been synonymous with civic and social life in the Western world since the time of Aristotle's *Politico*.[7] Notions of the proprietary, dwelling and 'the myth of architectural permanence' have been similarly privileged within Western architectural discourse '[f]or more than two millennia'.[8] As such, architecture is the built instantiation of systems of material wealth and 'property control – zoning, regulations, property laws, tax structures, moral and ethical positions on private and public property'.[9] These systems also have profound and often-underexamined implications for those who do not own property.

Meanwhile bodies are anathema to mainstream property systems because they neither own the buildings they inhabit nor determine the length of their stay in them. They exist in a state of betweenness, figuratively and literally between properties; complicating the legal, social and spatial enactment of the proprietary, and by extension, what is considered 'proper' in everyday society.[10] Despite, or indeed because of, their impropriety, temporary and nomadic bodies find their conceptual homes in philosophical discourses that embrace otherness: feminism, poststructuralism, post-humanism; discourses that affirm new spaces, typologies and positive 'figurations'[11] of the nomadic. Acknowledging the disparate and ambivalent lived realities of guardianship, we could argue that these nomadic figurations should not only invoke the joy of the temporary but be tethered to the more challenging aspects of ephemerality, precarity and the textures of vacant property decay.

Meanwhile bodies do slip into the urban and architectural discourses of temporary and tactical urbanism, artisanal and creative enterprise, and 'pop-up' retail.[12] In these discourses, their representation is complicated by their unlikely alliances with both grassroots community action and mainstream

Construction detail. The architecture of meanwhile bodies visualised as the well-worn suitcase in which they transport their lives and personal property.

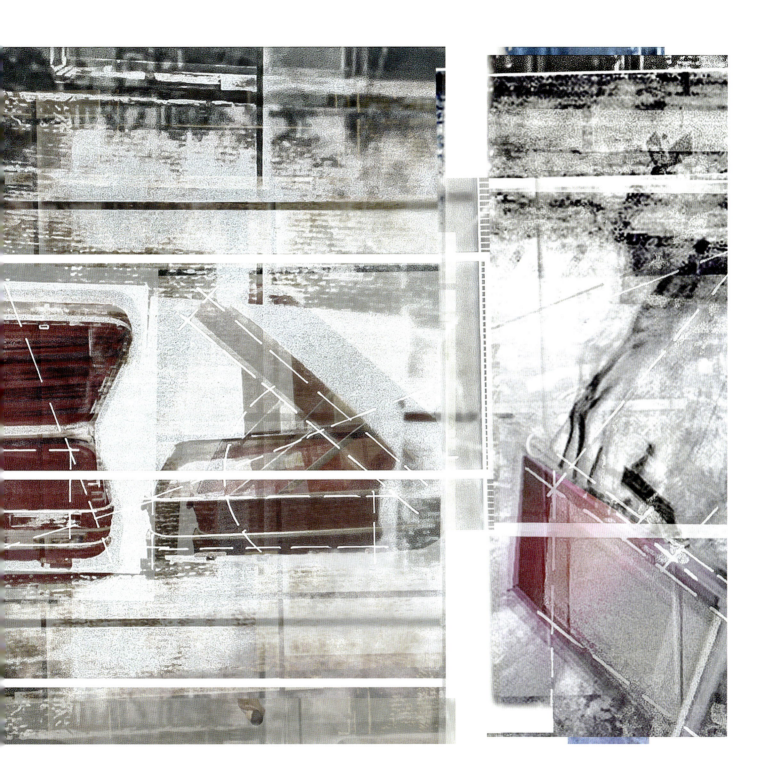

commerce. Instagram-worthy images celebrate the lifestyles and freedoms of digital nomads, the #vanlife movement, aligning the nomadic with consumerist choices. We also see the social and cultural aspirations of property guardians inhabiting spaces lovingly self-assembled from discarded and temporary materials – an architecture of productive refus(al), in a very literal sense. While inspiring for those without fixed abodes or large budgets, these overly positive images may also misrepresent the difficult lived realities of indeterminate accommodation (a point noted by guardians and providers alike). Notwithstanding most temporary tenure arrangements already prevent occupants from making significant alterations to the buildings they occupy, guardians also typically lack the funds and ability to update their spaces to the quality featured in social media feeds. When the practical challenges of temporary living intersect with a lack of affordable accommodation alternatives, meanwhile bodies can become stuck in transition, so to speak.

Meanwhile bodies are rendered nomadic by the unfortunate combination of social, political, environmental and economic forces that also influence our profession

Section. Meanwhile bodies traverse properties and property markets.

The Paradox of Meanwhile Architecture

Perhaps, therefore, the biggest challenge for meanwhile bodies relates to their ability to exit their temporary tenure. Meanwhile housing and property guardianship may be marketed as short-term accommodation solutions for individuals and sites in transition, but many guardians struggle financially to enter other longer-term accommodation arrangements, particularly in the same neighbourhoods. Thus, what was intended as temporary accommodation can, paradoxically, become a default tenure in perpetuity.

Responding to the needs of meanwhile bodies can lead to architectural solutions that appear as paradoxical as the tenure they support: simultaneously place-bound and location-independent, customised to each location but capable of disassembly and relocation at short notice. Intractable from the simultaneous conditions of emplacement and mobility, meanwhile architectures appear analogous to dwelling vessels in perpetual motion, hurtling across the time and space of urban regeneration – the resultant imagery potentially beguiling and problematic in equal measure. Meanwhile bodies are rendered nomadic by the unfortunate combination of social, political, environmental and economic forces that also influence our profession. While it may seem that we have limited influence over the flows of capital and property that produce meanwhile bodies, our architectural work is nonetheless embedded in them. As a profession, we need to recognise the rise of meanwhile bodies and their increasingly uncertain relationships with our built worlds. ᴆ

Notes

1. London Assembly Housing Committee, *Guardians in Occupation: Protecting London's Property Guardians*, Greater London Authority (London), February 2018, p 14.
2. Tino Buchholz, 'To Use or Not Use Urban Space', *4th International Conference of the International Forum on Urbanism (IFOU): The New Urban Question – Urbanism Beyond Neo-Liberalism*, Amsterdam/Delft, 2009, p 215; Mara Ferreri, Gloria Dawson and Alexander Vasudevan, 'Living Precariously: Property Guardianship and the Flexible City', *Transactions of the Institute of British Geographers*, 42 (2), 2016, p 251.
3. London Assembly Housing Committee, *op cit*, p 4.
4. For examples, see Studio Bark's The Shed Project, London, 2017: http://studiobark.co.uk/urban-livings-big-problem-studio-bark-on-the-bbc/ and Jan Kattein Architects' Blue House Yard, London, 2018: www.jankattein.com/portfolio-item/blue-house-yard/.
5. *Crashing*, written and created by Phoebe Waller-Bridge, directed by George Kane, Big Talk Productions, 2016.
6. Jill Stoner, *Toward A Minor Architecture*, MIT Press (Cambridge, MA), 2012, p 14; Catherine Ingraham, *Architecture and the Burdens of Linearity*, Yale University Press (New Haven, CT and London), 1998, pp 31–2; Fulcrum (ed), *Real Estates: Life Without Debt*, AA Publications/Bedford Press (London), 2015.
7. Stephen David Ross, *The Gift of Property: Having the Good*, State University of New York Press (New York), 2001; Nicholas Blomley, *Unsettling the City: Urban Land and the Politics of Property*, Routledge (London), 2004.
8. Stoner, *op cit*, p 14.
9. Ingraham, *op cit*, p 51.
10. Elizabeth Grosz, *Architecture from the Outside: Essays on Virtual and Real Space*, Writing Architecture Series, MIT Press (Cambridge, MA), 2011; Rosi Braidotti, *The Posthuman*, Polity Press (Cambridge), 2015, p 164.
11. Rosi Braidotti, *Nomadic Subjects: Embodiment and Sexual Difference in Contemporary Feminist Theory*, Columbia University Press (New York), 1994, p 3.
12. Mara Ferreri, 'The Seductions of Temporary Urbanism', *Ephemera: Theory and Politics in Organisation*, 15 (1), 2015, p 183; Peter Bishop and Lesley Williams, *The Temporary City*, Routledge (London), 2012, p 72.

Text © 2022 John Wiley & Sons Ltd. Images © Cathy Smith

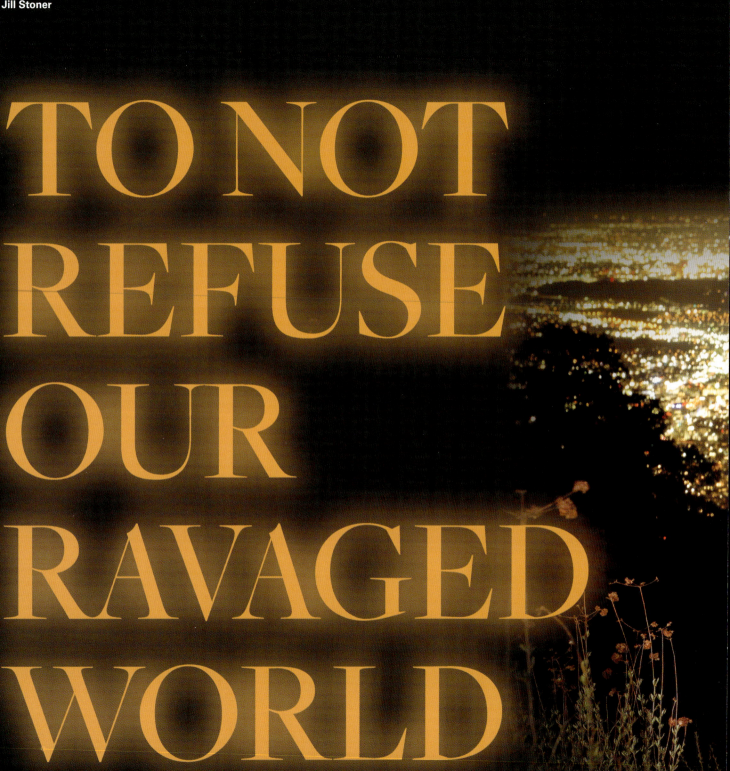

In a wide-ranging and pithy article, Guest-Editor of this issue and Professor at the Graduate School of the University of California, Berkeley, **Jill Stoner** evokes humanity, rivers, dogs and language to present a case for an architecture of refusal that allows us the possibility of 'breathing together'.

Imagine a river, but not just any river.[1] Not the glorious Whanganui in New Zealand, for millennia intertwined with the lives of Māori people and, since being granted personhood in 2017, represented by them in court. Not the Colorado River as it used to be before the Hoover Dam: a continuous ribbon made silver by sunlight, 1,450 miles (2,333 kilometres) long, wending its way from the high Rockies to the Pacific. Not any of the rivers that claim to set standards of purity for how all rivers should be.

Instead, imagine the Colorado as it has been for the last 100 years, channelled, dammed and diverted, boxed in concrete, much of it for most of the year as dry as old bones. Or the Tuolumne, a marvel of hydro-engineering made holy in an essay by Joan Didion.[2] Or the toxic Ganges, life-giving to hundreds of millions. For these rivers, there can be no return.

Wolves
Among the lasting images of the quarantine spring of 2020 are those of the animals. Long dispersed into the hinterlands by forces of human expansion, but emboldened by our pandemic retreat, they ventured forth to reclaim their former ground. Cougars roamed the streets of Santiago, Chile, families of wild boar hung out in empty parking lots in Haifa, Israel, and countless other sightings flooded social media around the world. Perhaps the animals came to reclaim their territory, our cities, and bravely remind us that we too are at risk. When people in the urban neighbourhoods of Northern Italy emerged onto their modest balconies to sing a cappella into the twilight sky, it was as if they found harmonies with wolves coming down from the hills.

Some of these reported sightings were exaggerated, and called out as evidence of our post-truth times.[3] But we can refuse to read these media fictions as lies. Like children's stories, imagining animals as independent actors in a human-constructed world de-masters and remakes that world into a deep well of possibility, a source of hope and liquid action.

Words
Ever since the Proto-Indo-European (PIE) language began to branch into tributaries, accumulating and redistributing material along its way, developing through the ages, words too have flowed freely from their sources. But part of the colonial project has been to remove words from that meandering temporality, to capture, pollute and condense them into commodities, to make verbs into nouns the better to fortify our illusion of progress and feed our cultural excess.

This Orwellian appropriation of language has turned (for example) the languid French verb *developer* into 'the developer', a hard, ruthless noun of a man, a speculator who drains wetlands for profit. But for those of us who studied ballet, *developer* brings to mind the *developpé*, a classic dance movement whereby the pointed toe is brought up to the knee, then fluidly unfolded into horizontal extension. Or, photographers might think of the slow development of images in the darkroom's red glow, as chemicals release captured light from paper.

Within this immediate context of 'architectures of refusal', consider the words 'complicity' and 'accomplice'. It is now common to speak of our profession's complicity in perpetuating systemic racism and spatial injustice, in resource exploitation and environmental degradation, in neoliberalism's grand project of profit at any cost. Even in general usage, complicity has become pejorative, wherein accomplices are fellow villains and nefarious actors assisting in some sort of crime. Yet the PIE root of complicity is *plek-*, meaning, simply, 'to braid', which is itself an extended form of the root *pel-*: 'to fold' or 'to bend'. Complicity is simply a complexity of folds.

We can take these words back, and allow them to continue to evolve. We can refuse to use them as they have been used. Reclaimed, they can contribute to productive discourse, take us to non-binary linguistic deltas and estuaries where multiplicities thrive and boundaries dissolve, in what poet Dionne Brand calls 'the whole immaculate language of a ravaged world'.[4] Here lie clues to possible futures where the constructed landscape becomes complicit and complicated, blurring its own edges, welcoming other species as accomplices while at the same time attending to its own unfolding.

Jill Stoner, *Crossings in a Ravaged World*, 'Ravaged World' series, 2022

Acknowledging no limits, in 2020 the Covid-19 pandemic crossed every imaginable geographical and architectural boundary. But it led to other crossings as well – crossings of lines that never really existed, between our carefully constructed environment and the territories of other species.

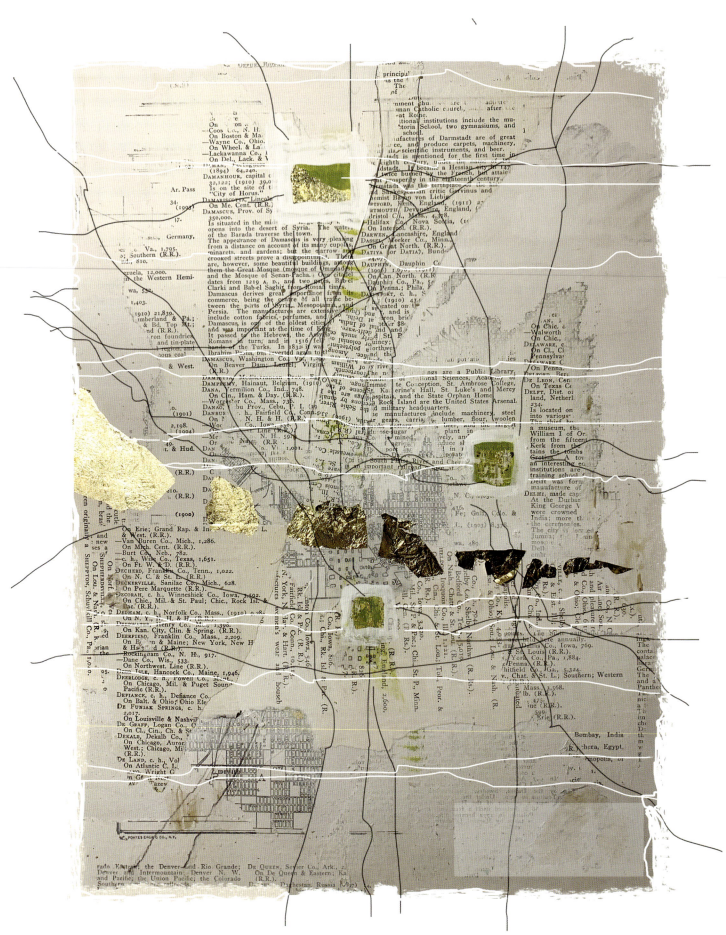

Jill Stoner,
Wanderings through a Ravaged World,
'Ravaged World' series,
2022

left: If we were to draw a temporal map of Elizabeth Lo's film *Stray* (2021), it would include not only the path she took with the dog actors each day, but the extravagant wanderings of all of the dogs. Their human connections would lead us back to the courtyards of the city, and their feral memories out to the urban margins.

Jill Stoner,
Inventory of a Ravaged World,
'Ravaged World' series,
2022

right: Dionne Brand's book-length poem *Inventory* takes us through the complex landscapes of terrorism, racism and climate change, weaving together the architectural excess of late capitalism with stories of those who suffer the consequences of that excess.

125

The Dogs of Istanbul

Until the mid-19th century, Ottoman citizens spent nearly all of their time indoors, and the streets of Istanbul belonged to their dogs. They announced intruders, warned of fire and cleared the streets of garbage. In return, they received food, shelter and health care. When European influences and authority claimed Istanbul in the late 19th century, the dogs were banished to offshore islands. In 1911, 80,000 dogs were infamously exiled to Sivriada, where they died of hunger and thirst or by drowning in their effort to escape. Their persecution, like that of Indigenous people in North America, was in effect a project to exterminate subjectivities, a colonial project of sterilisation that cleaned the city of its canine strands. Yet the paradox of their exile is their striking return: the following year, a devastating earthquake was understood as punishment, and the dogs were humbly welcomed back.

Award-winning cinematographer Elizabeth Lo's 2021 documentary *Stray* opens with words from Diogenes: 'Human beings live artificially and hypocritically, and would do well to study the dog.'[5] The film follows today's dogs of Istanbul as they wander and remap their city – not as feral intruders but as legal citizens. (In effect, like the river in New Zealand, they have been granted personhood.) The film features Zeytin, Nazar and Kartal in starring roles; they are tour guides, jaywalkers, *Istanbullu*, and best friends to a pack of Syrian boys who also live on the street. To emphasise the authority of her subjects, Lo devised a rig that lowered her camera to dog's-eye level, a subtle yet important shift, like dropping the third, sixth and seventh notes of a major scale. *Stray* is a film in a minor key in the voice of minority citizens telling their own story.

> To emphasise the authority of her subjects, Lo devised a rig that lowered her camera to dog-eye level, a subtle yet important shift

Elizabeth Lo,
Still from *Stray*,
2021

Zeytin and Nazar take a pause from their extravagant wanderings, against the backdrop of Istanbul's architecture.

The word 'stray' (v) is a shortening of the Old French *estraier* ('to wander'), which in turn is derived from the Vulgar Latin *estragare* – a contraction of *estravagare*, meaning 'to wander outside'. The daily lives of the dogs of Istanbul is an extravagance not of things, but extravagance made spatial. Here is the potential for buildings and landscapes, humans and animals, rivers and words to refuse false masters and to conspire (from *conspirer*: 'to breath together') more freely. Perhaps some day wolves will join their canine cousins as another strand in the tilted and curving byways of the city, and we on our balconies will truly become their accomplices in song.

An impossible development? We might best refuse to think so.

Epilogue

When I wrote *Toward a Minor Architecture* (2012),[6] the world was in recovery not from a pandemic but from financial troubles. At the time, the climate crisis was evident to scientists, yet languished in the shadows of our cultural conversation. The emergency of that moment was not a warming planet, nor the pervasive effects of systemic racism, but the immediate inconvenience of economic recession. In the US, the illusion of equal opportunity was foreclosed along with millions of homes. Cities and suburbs were glutted with empty and half-finished buildings, which I framed as 'nature' awaiting a new mandate for architecture, rooted in strategies of subtraction, and a refusal to set new foundations.

Though I still advocate for a moratorium on new construction, I read my own book differently now. No longer just a theoretical hypothesis for architecture's next direction, it is a footnote to the joyful, active, real-world complicities of my fellow authors in this journal. ⌂

Notes

1. Paraphrasing co-guest-editor Ozayr Saloojee – see p 16 of this issue.
2. Joan Didion, 'Holy Water', in *The White Album*, Simon & Schuster (New York), 1977, pp 59–66.
3. For example: www.nationalgeographic.com/animals/article/coronavirus-pandemic-fake-animal-viral-social-media-posts.
4. Dionne Brand, *Inventory*, McClelland & Stewart (Toronto), 2006, p 41.
5. Elizabeth Lo, *Stray*, Magnolia Pictures release, produced by Argos, in association with Intuitive Pictures and Periferi Film, 2020.
6. Jill Stoner, *Toward a Minor Architecture*, MIT Press (Cambridge, MA), 2012.

Elizabeth Lo and dogs, *Stray* production image, November 2020

Each night after a day of filming, the dogs accompanied Lo back to her hostel. She was able to rendevous with them the next day through GPS tracking. This image shows the camera rig, which gives the film its unique 'dog's-eye' view of Istanbul.

Text © 2022 John Wiley & Sons Ltd. Images: pp 120–21 © Johanna Turner; pp 123–5 © Jill Stoner; pp 126–7 © Ellizabeth Lo

FROM ANOTHER PERSPECTIVE

A Word from *D* Editor Neil Spiller

Balking in the Balkans

Lebbeus Woods – *Zagreb Free Zone* Revisited

Lebbeus Woods, Zagreb Free Zone, 1991

Woods used electrostatic collages of drawings and contextual photographs to explore the scale, interior and placement of his freespaces.

> [A]rchitects must take the initiative, beginning from a point of origin that precedes anything to be resisted, one deep within an idea of architecture itself. They can never think of themselves as resisters, or join resistance movements, or preach resistance. Rather (and this is the hard part of resistance) they must create an independent idea of both architecture and the world.
> — Lebbeus Woods, 2009[1]

One of the most, if not the most seminal examples of the 'architecture of refusal' is Lebbeus Woods's Zagreb Free Zone project created in 1991 and exhibited at the Croatian city's Museum of Arts and Crafts from April to May that year. From March to April of 2021, it was once again exhibited in Zagreb, this time at the Oris gallery. It is a work that continues to resonate and will do so into the deep future.

The project commenced its gestation in 1989, the time of the fall of the Berlin Wall, but Woods's interest in the mystique and potential of Central and Eastern Europe had been sparked decades before. What began as an appreciation of the writers and filmmakers was then galvanised by listening to Russian novelist Alexander Solzhenitsyn's commencement address at Harvard, on the radio, in 1978.[2] The speech invoked the possibility that, if there were to be a renaissance in Europe, it would come out of this geographical area. So, when the invitation came from the Croatian capital, Zagreb, to project and possibly build a piece of the project, Woods was very excited.

Freespace and Free Zone

The late 1980s and the beginning of the 1990s were a period of many political and social shifts in the space then called the Socialist Federal Republic of Yugoslavia. Something new was emerging, but would it be beneficial for the people who lived there? Woods felt the need to work anew: '[It] was simply unacceptable that I should come to the Museum in Zagreb with anything less than a project for participation in that city's transformation.'[3]

He proposed a network of highly wrought 'freespace' structures existing within a 'Free Zone'. These concepts were already present in Woods's 1990 Free Zone project for Berlin.[4] However, Zagreb presents some radical differences. Here the 'freespace' buildings/objects are situated in the streets as catalysts for the evolution of a new set of social, political and domestic/personal conditions – questioning the established relationships between private and public spaces, and their function and form. They also question the economic expediency of building materiality and ways of making built enclosures. By the early 1990s, digital means of communication were burgeoning. Unsurprisingly, each 'freespace' intervention was proposed to contain all manner of electronic instrumentation within it – used depending on the personal preoccupations of each occupant. Such potential disruptions – good or bad, no one could know in advance – would inject architectural 'noise', both virtual and actual, into the rapidly changing situation in Zagreb. This interface would hopefully foster new ways to live, testing spatial norms and provoking new communal activities.

Free Zone is 'nothing more nor less than a series of shifting centres that disturb in a human way the great pool of electromagnetic energies comprising a global field of human and natural interactions'.[5] Each 'freespace' structure is an element within the 'Free Zone' network – a global matrix of human perception and experience. The 'freespace' interventions and enclosures were mobile, moved by helicopter, offering shelter for individuals rooted 'only in the strangely social isolation of their modernity'.[6]

The Cybernetic Circus
Zagreb Free Zone is predicated on Woods's railing against consumer society by making his work indigestible when seen through its distorted lens. The whole consuming nature of capitalism (the way it strips meaning from words and concepts, creates equivalences, nothingness, fakes and careless histories), and the refusal of it, was grist to Woods's creative mill and the emotional motive power behind this project. 'In a consumer society, the only recourse is to make one's work indigestible. Otherwise it will become the inevitable end product of all processes of consumption: excrement. Nothing is more indigestible than the concept or reality of freedom.'[7]

Second-order cybernetics, which conditioned Woods's perception of the world, determines that we individually 'build' a personal universe of discourse that is continually changing and readjusting as we interact with what is around us – emotionally, physically and philosophically. In the short and playful essay entitled 'Notes on the Cybernetic Circus',[8] written for the Zagreb exhibition catalogue of 1991, Woods links his understanding of cybernetics with freedom and the happy absurdity of circus performers. For him, circus acts are meaningless and useless, yet, precisely due to that, those who perform them are free. Human condition demands the pursuit of the absurd and the meaningless. If done with dedication, such a pursuit can result in freedom from the constraints of capitalism – and that is what the 'freespaces' are about.

Performance
In his introduction to the 2021 catalogue *Zagreb Free Zone – The Encore Performance*, the Croatian architect Leo Modrčin, Woods's sometime collaborator and a conduit for the Zagreb 1991 exhibition, states that this project 'remains an ultimate architectural performance … grounded in the transformative potential of architecture'.[9]

Woods's spirally bound, rectangular sketchbooks could be conceived as theatrical scripts and stage

City plan showing structures and fluctuating electromagnetic fields, within which the freespaces were to be placed and moved.

Woods was very explicit about the interior arrangements of the freespaces but did not dictate their multiple possible programmes and functions.

Human condition demands the pursuit of the absurd and the meaningless. If done with dedication, such a pursuit can result in freedom from the constraints of capitalism – and that is what the 'freespaces' are about.

directions, a confluence of choreography and intellectual intent. They describe architectural placements of extraordinary composite, faceted objects in the cityscape as well as their internal spatial arrangements, often in one take, subscribing to hardly any traditional architectural protocols – indeed an architecture of refusal.

One sketchbook page elaborates the concept of the Cybernetic Circus and reinforces the theatrical nature of these structures combined with their mathematical exactitude. Modrčin quotes it at the end of his introduction to the 2021 catalogue volume: 'The performers make precise movements and gestures, essentially mathematical in nature. In fact, performers are mathematicians before anything else; masters of number(s) and also spaces between numbers. Harmonies, dissonances, frequencies fluctuating in cadences of transformation spontaneously devised and themselves transformed … .'[10] Modrčin asks us to reread the above quotation and the one that follows it while replacing the word 'performers' with the word 'architects'. In the same sketchbook entry, Woods continues: 'There is something cold in their performance, something detached and remote, resisting the pathos inherent in their actions. They detest pathos and are notoriously unsentimental; they are often accused of indifference and inadvertence, but never excuse themselves, explain or apologise.'[11] These passages of prose get right to the intellectual centre of the Zagreb project, describing its unapologetic difference.

Taking the City to Task
Some commentators have accused Woods of leaning to the political right due to his speculations being predicated on the self-determination of the individual, but this is not the case. Freespaces and the Free Zones are not allusions to the 'free' markets of unrestrained capitalism. The opposite is true. According to Woods, 'Freespace is not *demanded* by any of the existing cultural or social institutions, or even by an individual who has in mind for it some particular use. It does not belong to an existing building *type* which excludes it from the market place.'[12]

The Zagreb Free Zone could be said to occupy an extraordinary yet paradoxical position within avant-garde 'paper architecture'. Its uniqueness is born out of the initial request, to exhibit. The eruption of the war in June of 1991, and the subsequent disintegration of Yugoslavia, made the second step, proposed by the Museum of Arts and Crafts – to build a structure – unrealisable. The drawings and models are highly specific. Woods did not consider himself a paper architect. The precision with which he drew freespaces belies the intention to construct them. But to achieve them, Woods eschewed a strategy that many an architect would have adopted – the use of a ubiquitous isotropic grid – to achieve a level of adaptability.

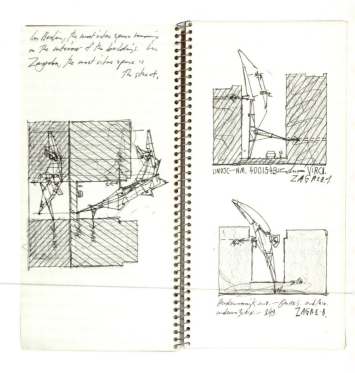

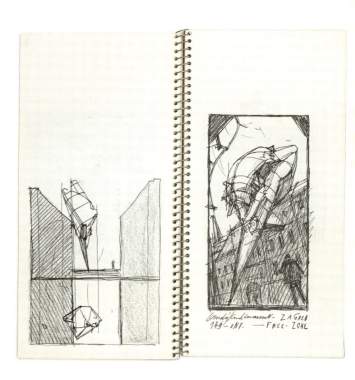

Woods's sketchbook shows the exactitude with which he posited ideas and forms. His linework is performative and theatrical.

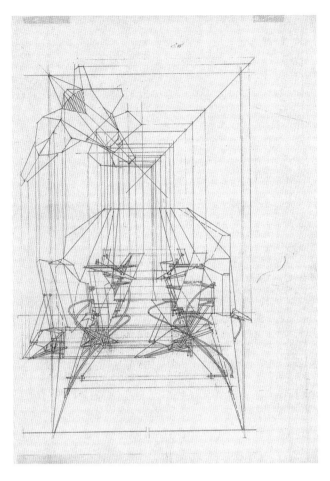

Woods started to make preliminary drawings for a built freespace structure in the garden of the Museum of Arts and Crafts, but the outbreak of war halted the endeavour.

Woods believed that the use of the grid in much contemporary architecture was symbiotically linked to the mediocrity of much of the work done in them

The grid predicates much modern architecture with its plug-in-and-play service nodes and prefabricated partitions: 'The Cartesian grid … is not precise, rather it is a generalised abstraction. As a spatial and formal construct, it has no character, and therefore can be occupied without character, a fact [to which] too many … buildings testify.'[13]

Woods believed that the use of the grid in much contemporary architecture was symbiotically linked to the mediocrity of much of the work done in them and that it leads to the degradation of the human spirit. In this sense, the freespaces and zones not only speculate on a possible future for Zagreb, but represent a call for re-evaluation of all existing cities and social structures. The Postmodern condition, even more exacerbated in the 30 years since Woods first drew his propositions, continually asks us to dwell on an 'anarchical landscape of emptied meaning and voided authority'.[14] It is this, political, questioning that is as important as Woods's beautifully honed drawings and expressive models: it is their lifeblood. ⌂

Notes

1. Lebbeus Woods, 'Architecture and Resistance', 9 May 2009: https://lebbeuswoods.wordpress.com/2009/05/09/architecture-and-resistance/.
2. Alexander Solzhenitsyn, 'A World Split Apart', speech delivered at Harvard University, 8 June 1978: www.americanrhetoric.com/speeches/alexandersolzhenitsynharvard.htm.
3. Lebbeus Woods, 'Zagreb-Free-Zone: A Memoir' (18 June 1991), republished in Leo Modrčin, Lovorka Prpić and Aleksandra Wagner (eds), *Lebbeus Woods: Zagreb Free Zone Revisited*, exh cat, University of Zagreb Faculty of Architecture and Oris House of Architecture (Zagreb), 2021, p 32.
4. Kristin Feireiss (ed), *Lebbeus Woods, FREE-ZONE-BERLIN: Entwurf für das Zentrum der Metropole*, exh cat, Aedes (Berlin), 1991.
5. Woods, 'Zagreb-Free-Zone: A Memoir', *op cit*.
6. *Ibid*.
7. Lebbeus Woods, 'Notes on the Cybernetic Circus' (1991), republished in Modrčin, Prpić and Wagner (eds), *op cit*, p 10.
8. *Ibid*.
9. Leo Modrčin in Modrčin, Prpić and Wagner (eds), *op cit*, p 2.
10. *Ibid*, p 4.
11. Lebbeus Woods, 'Notes on the Cybernetic Circus', sketchbook page, dated 7 June 1991, Zagreb.
12. Lebbeus Woods, 'Come the Revolution: Anarchitecture – Architecture is a Political Act', Academy Editions (London), 1992, republished in Modrčin, Prpić and Wagner (eds), *op cit*, p 53.
13. *Ibid*, p 54.
14. *Ibid*.

Text © 2022 John Wiley & Sons Ltd. Images: p 128 © Robbie Munn; pp 129–33 © Estate of Lebbeus Woods

ARCHITECTURES OF REFUSAL

Piper Bernbaum is an assistant professor at the Azrieli School of Architecture and Urbanism at Carleton University in Canada. She is the recipient of the Canadian Prix de Rome for Emerging Practitioners, and the Governor Generals Academic Gold Medal of Canada. Her research is focused on the intersection of law and architecture, the considerations and constraints of social and spatial plurality, and the appropriation of space through design.

Carwil Bjork-James is Assistant Professor of Anthropology at Vanderbilt University in Nashville, Tennessee, and author of *The Sovereign Street: Making Revolution in Urban Bolivia* (University of Arizona Press, 2020). He conducts immersive and historical research on disruptive protest, environmental struggles, state violence and indigenous collective rights in Bolivia. His work draws on his experience as a human rights advocate for oil-affected communities and as a participant in direct action protest movements. He is currently principal investigator on Ultimate Consequences, a comprehensive database of people killed in Bolivian political conflict since 1982.

Tom Carruthers is an architect, artist and co-founder of Dream The Combine, a creative studio that has produced numerous site-specific installations in the US and Canada. He is Assistant Professor of the Practice at the College of Architecture, Art, and Planning (AAP) at Cornell University in Ithaca, New York. He is the winner of the 2022 United States Artists Fellowship in Architecture and Design; 2021 McKnight Fellowship for Visual Artists; 2020–21 J Irwin and Xenia S Miller Prize; 2018 Young Architects Program at MoMA PS1; 2018 Art Omi Architecture Residency; and 2017 FSP/Jerome Foundation Fellowship, and is co-curator of the 2023 Counterpublic Triennial in St Louis, Missouri. Dream The Combine also won the 2022–23 Rome Prize in Architecture from the American Academy in Rome.

Thireshen Govender is an architect, urbanist and researcher practising in Johannesburg, South Africa. Following a Master's in Urban Design at the Bartlett School of Architecture, University College London (UCL), he founded UrbanWorks, a design-research studio concerned with the design and implementation of transformative infrastructures on post-traumatic sites. He is the co-author of *Township Economies: People, Spaces, Practices* (HSRC Press, 2020). His research through the University of Johannesburg's Graduate School of Architecture, where he led Unit 14: Rogue Economies, documents the hidden forces shaping our cities while experimenting with methods on radical speculation in the context of extreme urban crisis.

Lucía Jalón Oyarzun is an architect and researcher. She graduated from the ETSAM School of Architecture of Madrid where she also completed her PhD 'Exception and the rebel body: the political as generator of a minor architecture' in 2017. She is currently Head of Research at Atelier de la Conception de l'Espace (ALICE) at the École polytechnique fédérale de Lausanne (EPFL) and a research fellow at the Center of Digital Visual Studies at the University of Zurich, where she continues her interdisciplinary research on minor architectures.

Jennifer Newsom is an architect, artist and co-founder of Dream The Combine, and Assistant Professor at Cornell AAP. She is winner of the 2022 United States Artists Fellowship in Architecture and Design; 2021 McKnight Fellowship for Visual Artists; 2020–21 J Irwin and Xenia S Miller Prize; 2018 Young Architects Program at MoMA PS1; 2018 Art Omi Architecture Residency; and the 2017 FSP/Jerome Foundation Fellowship. She is also co-curator of the 2023 Counterpublic Triennial in St Louis, Missouri.

Thompson Cong Nguyen is an architectural designer and a child of Vietnamese refugees who grew up in suburban Mississauga, Ontario, Canada. He has lived and worked in Toronto where he made spaces of belonging through advocating, designing and partying with fellow queer and racialised friends in the city. He is a recent graduate of the MArch programme at the Azrieli School of Architecture and Urbanism at Carleton University.

Quilian Riano is Interim Dean of Pratt Institute's School of Architecture in Brooklyn, New York, working across the school's architecture, landscape and planning programmes to develop and manage pedagogical projects and partnerships. He has over a decade of teaching experience and is a core member of the Dark Matter University (DMU). He is also the founder of DSGN AGNC, a studio exploring politically driven design, processes and engagements through architecture, urbanism, landscapes and art. He holds a Bachelors of Design in Architecture

CONTRIBUTORS

(BDes) from the University of Florida's School of Architecture and a Masters of Architecture (MArch) from Harvard University's Graduate School of Design (GSD).

Hannah le Roux is an architect and historian of modern architecture in Southern Africa. Her current research projects are the toxic legacies of asbestos-cement products and mining residues, in and beyond the Witwatersrand township; the materialisation of black low-cost housing by white architects during apartheid; and the Africa volume of the *Bloomsbury Global Encyclopaedia of Women in Architecture*. She is an Associate Professor at the University of the Witwatersrand.

Alberto de Salvatierra is founder and director of the Center for Civilization and assistant professor of urbanism and data in architecture at the University of Calgary School of Architecture, Planning and Landscape (SAPL) in Alberta, Canada. An interdisciplinary polymath, architectural designer and landscape urbanist, his research and work focuses on material flows as infrastructure at the urban and civilisational scales, and also within the broader frameworks of planetary urbanisation, landscape as urbanism, and vernacular architecture. He holds a Bachelor of Architecture from Cornell University, and both a Master of Landscape Architecture and Master of Design Studies in Urbanism, Landscape and Ecology from Harvard University's GSD.

Cathy Smith is an Australian architect, interior designer and Senior Lecturer in Interior Architecture at the University of New South Wales in Sydney, Australia, where she has also been the inaugural Turnbull Foundation Women in Built Environment scholar. She was a Richard Rogers Fellow (Harvard University GSD, autumn 2018), and Visiting Professor at Carleton University (winter 2019 and 2020). Her design practice and interdisciplinary scholarly research concentrate on issues of social equity, property tenure, placemaking and urban renewal, and particularly the DIY procurement methodology of meanwhile interiors and architecture, and has been published in a mixture of industry and scholarly journals.

Neil Spiller is Editor of *D*, and was previously Hawksmoor Chair of Architecture and Landscape and Deputy Pro Vice Chancellor at the University of Greenwich in London. Prior to this he was Vice Dean at the Bartlett School of Architecture, UCL. He has made an international reputation as an architect, designer, artist, teacher, writer and polemicist. He is the founding director of the Advanced Virtual and Technological Architecture Research (AVATAR) group, which continues to push the boundaries of architectural design and discourse in the face of the impact of 21st-century technologies. Its current preoccupations include augmented and mixed realities and other metamorphic technologies.

Chat Travieso is an artist and designer, as well as co-founder of the multidisciplinary collaborative practice Yeju & Chat, with Yeju Choi. He is an adjunct assistant professor at Columbia University's Graduate School of Architecture, Planning and Preservation (GSAPP), a part-time faculty member at Parsons School of Design, and a visiting assistant professor at Pratt Institute. He creates participatory, architectural and research-based projects that reinforce social bonds in public spaces and interrogate the history and policies that have shaped our built environment. He holds a BFA from the Maryland Institute College of Art and an MArch from the Yale School of Architecture.

Ilze Wolff is an architect working in Cape Town. With Heinrich Wolff, she co-directs Wolff Architects, a practice that is concerned with developing an architecture of consequence. She is the author of *Unstitching Rex Trueform: The Story of an African Factory* (2017), an interdisciplinary study of a modernist garment manufacturing factory in Salt River, Cape Town. Her main preoccupation as an architect is to reconstruct and seek out spatialities of collective freedom. Her belief in the ancient technology of storytelling finds its way in various forms of expression: architecture, creative non-fiction writing, mothering, film, gardening, teaching and prophetic organising.

What is *Architectural Design*?

Founded in 1930, *Architectural Design* (⌂) is an influential and prestigious publication. It combines the currency and topicality of a newsstand journal with the rigour and production qualities of a book. With an almost unrivalled reputation worldwide, it is consistently at the forefront of cultural thought and design.

Issues of ⌂ are edited either by the journal Editor, Neil Spiller, or by an invited Guest-Editor. Renowned for being at the leading edge of design and new technologies, ⌂ also covers themes as diverse as architectural history, the environment, interior design, landscape architecture and urban design.

Provocative and pioneering, ⌂ inspires theoretical, creative and technological advances. It questions the outcome of technical innovations as well as the far-reaching social, cultural and environmental challenges that present themselves today.

For further information on ⌂, subscriptions and purchasing single issues see:

https://onlinelibrary.wiley.com/journal/15542769

Individual backlist issues of ⌂ are available as books for purchase starting at £29.99 / US$45.00

www.wiley.com

How to Subscribe
With 6 issues a year, you can subscribe to ⌂ (either print, online or through the ⌂ App for iPad)

Institutional subscription
£357 / US$666
online only

£373 / US$695
print only

£401 / US$748
print and online

Personal-rate subscription
£151 / US$236
print and iPad access

Student-rate subscription
£97 / US$151
print only

⌂ App for iPad
6-issue subscription:
£44.99 / US$64.99
Individual issue:
£9.99 / US$13.99

To subscribe to print or online
E: cs-journals@wiley.com
W: https://onlinelibrary.wiley.com/journal/15542769

Americas
E: cs-journals@wiley.com
T: +1 877 762 2974

Europe, Middle East and Africa
E: cs-journals@wiley.com
T: +44 (0)18 6577 8315

Asia Pacific
E: cs-journals@wiley.com
T: +65 6511 8000

Japan (for Japanese-speaking support)
E: cs-japan@wiley.com
T: +65 6511 8010

Visit our Online Customer Help
available in 7 languages at www.wileycustomerhelp.com/ask

Volume 91 No 6
ISBN 978 1119 812241

Volume 92 No 1
ISBN 978 1119 743255

Volume 92 No 2
ISBN 978 1119 748793

Volume 92 No 3
ISBN 978 1119 748847

Volume 92 No 4
ISBN 978 1119 787778

Volume 92 No 5
ISBN 978 1119 833762

⌂ NOW available on the iPad!

- Buy single issues or subscribe
- Store all downloaded issues to your personal library
- Easily navigable format brings new life to ⌂ articles
- Free to personal print subscribers

Available on the App Store